The Time Machine Chronicles: Old Testament Characters

Joshua Rhoades

Published by Joshua Paul Rhoades, 2024.

THE TIME MACHINE CHRONICLES: OLD TESTAMENT CHARACTERS

First edition. August 31, 2024.

Copyright © 2024 Joshua Rhoades.

ISBN: 979-8227339324

Written by Joshua Rhoades.

Also by Joshua Rhoades

Courage Under Fire: David's Stand On The Battlefield
Jonah's Journey: Voices Of Redemption And Lessons In Obedience
The Furnace Of Faith: 12 Principles From The Heat Of Faith
Whispers of Hope: Inspiring Stories of Men's Prayers In Scripture
Frontier Legends: The Oregon Dream
Elijah: A Beacon Of Boldness
HOOK, LINE & SAVIOUR - Faith Reflections from Fishing
Driven By Faith: Motor Racing Inspired Christian Life
30 Day Devotional - Bold and Strong- Coffee Devotions for a
Courageous Christian Walk
Authentic Christianity: The Heart of Old Time Religion
Consider The Ant - God's Tiny Preachers
Flee Fornication: The Plea For Purity
Renewed Hope- How to Find Encouragement in God
Sounding The Call - The Voice of Conviction
The Altar - Where Heaven Meets Earth
The Bible's Battlefields- Timeless Lessons from Ancient Wars
The Sacred Art of Silence - How Silence Speaks in Scripture
Under Fire- The Sanctity of the Traditional Biblical Home
Who Is on the Lord's Side? A Call to Righteousness
What Is Truth? - From Skepticism to Submission
First and Goal- Faith and Football Fundamentals
From Dugout to Devotion- Spiritual Lessons from Baseball
Par for the Course- Faith and Fairways
The Believer's Pace- Tools for Running Life's Marathon

The Immutable Fortress- Security in God's Unchanging Nature
Biblical Bravery
Deer Stands and Devotions: A Hunter's Walk with God
Jesus Knows- Our Hearts, Our Responsibility
Restoration - Setting The Bone
Spiritual 911- God's Word for Life's Emergency's
The Freedom of Forgiveness
The Jezebel Effect - Ancient Manipulations Modern Lessons
The Shout That Stopped The Saviour
The Time Machine Chronicles: Old Testament Characters

Introduction

Welcome to "The Time Machine Chronicles: Old Testament Characters," where four adventurous children—James, Mary, David, and Linda—embark on an incredible journey through time. With the help of a mysterious time machine they discover in an old attic, they travel back thousands of years to witness firsthand the lives of iconic figures from the Old Testament. Each adventure brings these biblical stories to life, teaching the children—and readers—timeless lessons that resonate in our world today.

Their first stop is Noah's time, where they watch him build the ark despite being ridiculed by others. James, who has been struggling with doubt, learns the importance of trusting God, even when the task seems impossible. This encounter with Noah's unwavering faith inspires James to place his trust in God's plan for his life.

Next, they journey to meet Abraham and Sarah in Canaan. As they witness God's promise of a son being fulfilled, Mary, who's been searching for purpose, learns to trust in God's timing. Abraham and Sarah's story helps her understand that God's promises are always reliable, even when they require patience and faith.

The adventure continues as they stand alongside young David on the battlefield, facing Goliath. Watching David's courage and trust in God, the young David in our story learns that with God's help, he can overcome his own fears and challenges.

Finally, they travel to Egypt, where they witness Joseph's trials and triumphs. Linda, who has been struggling with forgiveness, is deeply moved by Joseph's ability to forgive his brothers. Through Joseph's example, she learns the power of forgiveness and the importance of trusting God's plan.

"The Time Machine Chronicles: Old Testament Characters" invites you to join James, Mary, David, and Linda on their journey, discovering timeless biblical truths that can transform your life today.

Chapter 1 - Creation of the World

James, Mary, David, and Linda were playing in their backyard one sunny afternoon when they stumbled upon an old, mysterious machine buried under some leaves. Intrigued, they wiped off the dirt and discovered a time machine. With a mix of excitement and curiosity, they decided to try it out. The machine whirred to life, and before they knew it, they were whisked away to a time long before humans roamed the earth. They found themselves in complete darkness, hovering in space, as a booming voice said, "Let there be light." Suddenly, light burst forth, separating day from night. They watched in awe as God created the heavens and the earth, shaping the land and seas, and filling them with plants and trees of every kind. Each day brought something new and incredible. On the second day, they saw the sky being formed, separating the waters above from the waters below. The sky was a brilliant blue, stretching endlessly above them. On the third day, they marveled as dry land appeared, and God covered it with lush greenery, from towering trees to delicate flowers. The kids could almost smell the fresh, fragrant blooms and feel the cool, damp soil beneath their feet.

The fourth day was even more spectacular as they witnessed the creation of the sun, moon, and stars. They watched in amazement as God placed the sun in the sky to rule the day and the moon and stars to illuminate the night. The sky was now filled with twinkling stars, and the children felt a sense of wonder at the vastness of the universe. On the fifth day, the seas and skies came alive with creatures. They saw enormous whales swimming gracefully in the oceans and colorful fish darting through coral reefs. Birds of every kind soared through the sky, their songs filling the air with a symphony of life. James pointed out a majestic eagle, while Mary marveled at the delicate hummingbirds flitting among the flowers.

The sixth day was perhaps the most exciting. The children watched as God created animals to fill the earth—lions, elephants, horses, and so many more. Each animal was unique and beautiful in its own way. Then, in a moment that took their breath away, they saw God form a man from the dust of the ground and breathe life into him. Adam, the first human, came to life. God then created Eve from one of Adam's ribs, and together they were placed in the Garden of Eden, a paradise on earth. The garden was more beautiful than anything the children had ever seen. It was filled with vibrant plants, clear streams, and gentle animals. The children stepped into the garden and felt the soft grass under their feet and the warm sun on their faces. They approached Adam and Eve, who greeted them with smiles and kind words. Adam and Eve explained that they were to care for the garden and all the creatures within it. They spoke of their special relationship with God, who walked with them in the garden in the cool of the day. The children felt a deep sense of peace and joy in the Garden of Eden. They played with the animals, tasted the sweet fruits from the trees, and explored the lush landscape. They felt a connection to the creation all around them and to Adam and Eve, who treated them like friends. As the sun set on the sixth day, the children noticed a sense of completeness and harmony in the garden. They realized that God had created everything with a purpose and that each part of creation was interconnected. On the seventh day, God rested, and the children felt a profound sense of rest and contentment as well. They sat with Adam and Eve, enjoying the beauty and tranquility of the garden.

However, the time machine began to hum, signaling that it was time to return home. Reluctantly, they said their goodbyes to Adam and Eve, thanking them for sharing their story. They stepped back into the time machine, and with a whirl and a flash, they were transported back to their backyard. The adventure left a lasting impression on James, Mary, David, and Linda. They talked excitedly about all they had seen and learned. They felt a new appreciation for the world around them and a deeper understanding of the beauty and complexity of God's creation. They knew that they had witnessed something truly extraordinary, a glimpse into the very beginning of the world.

Back home, they couldn't wait to share their incredible journey with their families. They spent hours recounting every detail, from the creation of light to their time in the Garden of Eden. Their families listened with amazement, and the children's excitement was infectious. They decided to document their adventure, creating a journal filled with drawings and descriptions of what they had seen. Each page captured a different day of creation, and their accounts were so vivid that it felt like reliving the experience. The children made a pact to cherish the world around them and to remember the lessons they had learned from their time-traveling adventure. They felt a deep sense of responsibility to care for the earth and its creatures, just as Adam and Eve were tasked with caring for the Garden of Eden.

Their adventure to the beginning of the world had ignited a curiosity and wonder in the children that would stay with them for the rest of their lives. They often returned to their journal, reading their stories and looking at their drawings, reminding themselves of the incredible journey they had taken. They knew that their time machine held many more adventures and that there were countless other stories to discover in the pages of history. But for now, they were content with the memories of their first journey, a journey that had taken them to the dawn of creation and back again. They looked forward to the future with excitement, knowing that with each new adventure, they would learn more about the world and their place in it.

Chapter 2 - Noah's Ark

James, Mary, David, and Linda could hardly contain their excitement as they gathered around the time machine in their backyard once again. Their first adventure to witness the creation of the world had left them in awe, and they were eager to see what their next journey would bring. With a quick check to ensure everything was set, they entered the coordinates for a new destination: the time of Noah. The machine hummed to life, and within moments, they found themselves standing in the midst of a bustling construction site. All around them, people were working tirelessly, hauling massive wooden beams and hammering nails into place. The air was filled with the sounds of sawing, hammering, and the occasional shout of instruction. At the center of it all stood a colossal wooden structure that dwarfed everything around it—the ark.

Noah, a sturdy man with a kind face and strong hands, was overseeing the work. His sons, Shem, Ham, and Japheth, worked alongside him, their muscles straining as they lifted heavy planks and secured them into place. The children watched in amazement as the massive ark took shape before their eyes. Noah noticed the children standing nearby and walked over to greet them. "Hello there," he said with a warm smile. "What brings you to our construction site?" James, always the spokesperson for the group, stepped forward and explained that they were travelers from a distant land, eager to learn about the great project Noah was undertaking. Noah nodded, understanding in his eyes. "God has commanded me to build this ark," he explained. "A great flood is coming to cleanse the earth of its wickedness, and this ark will save my family and a pair of every kind of animal."

The children listened intently as Noah described the divine instructions he had received and the ridicule he faced from his neighbors. Many people thought Noah was mad for building such a massive ship on dry land, but Noah's faith remained unshaken. He believed in God's promise and was determined to complete the task, no matter the cost. As they spent time with Noah and his family, the children marveled at their dedication and hard work. They watched as the ark slowly took shape, its wooden hull towering above them. The children even helped in small ways, carrying tools and fetching water for the workers. They felt a sense of purpose and camaraderie as they contributed to the monumental effort.

Days turned into weeks, and the ark was finally complete. It was a magnificent structure, stretching as far as the eye could see, with three decks and ample space for all the animals that would soon arrive. The children were amazed by the sheer size and complexity of the ark, and they could hardly believe that it had been built by hand, with only the simplest of tools. One day, as the sky darkened with heavy clouds, Noah received a message from God: it was time to gather the animals and prepare for the flood. The children watched in awe as pairs of animals began to arrive from all directions. Lions and lambs, elephants and eagles, all marched into the ark in a peaceful procession, guided by an unseen hand. It was a sight unlike anything the children had ever seen.

With the animals safely aboard, Noah's family and the children entered the ark. As they secured the massive door, the first drops of rain began to fall. The pitter-patter on the wooden roof soon grew into a torrential downpour, and the ground outside quickly became a churning sea of mud and water. The ark creaked and groaned as it began to lift off the ground, buoyed by the rising floodwaters. Inside, the children huddled together, their hearts pounding with a mix of fear and excitement. They could hear the roar of the storm outside, the relentless pounding of rain and the howling wind. The ark rocked back and forth, sometimes violently, but Noah remained calm, his faith unshaken. He assured everyone that God was with them and would see them safely through the storm.

Days turned into weeks as the ark floated on the endless sea. The children marveled at the vastness of the floodwaters, which stretched out in every direction, as far as the eye could see. They helped care for the animals, feeding them and cleaning their enclosures, and they grew closer to Noah's family, learning about their faith and resilience. They also witnessed the harmony between the animals, who seemed to sense the gravity of their situation and remained calm and peaceful throughout the journey. One day, after many weeks adrift, the rain finally stopped. The clouds began to part, revealing a bright blue sky. The sun's warm rays felt like a blessing after so long in the dark and damp. Noah released a raven, which flew back and forth but found no place to land. Then he released a dove, but it too returned, finding no resting place.

After seven days, Noah released the dove again, and this time it returned with a freshly plucked olive leaf in its beak. The children cheered at the sight, understanding that the waters were receding and that land was once again emerging. They watched eagerly as the ark slowly drifted toward a mountaintop and came to rest on solid ground. It was Mount Ararat. The children could hardly contain their excitement as Noah opened the door of the ark, and they stepped out onto dry land. The air was fresh and clean, and the sight of the green hills and blooming flowers filled their hearts with joy. The animals began to leave the ark, bounding into the new world with renewed energy and vigor.

Noah and his family built an altar and offered a sacrifice of thanksgiving to God, who had saved them from the flood. The children joined in the prayers, feeling a deep sense of gratitude and awe for the divine protection they had experienced. God placed a rainbow in the sky, a sign of His covenant with Noah and all living creatures, promising never to destroy the earth with a flood again. The children gazed at the brilliant colors of the rainbow, understanding the significance of God's promise and the hope it represented for the future.

As the time machine signaled that it was time to return home, the children said their goodbyes to Noah and his family. They thanked them for their hospitality and the invaluable lessons they had learned during their time together. With a final look at the ark and the beautiful rainbow arching over the landscape, they stepped into the time machine and set the coordinates for home. The journey back felt shorter, and soon they were standing in their familiar backyard once again. They were filled with a sense of accomplishment and wonder, knowing they had witnessed one of the most significant events in biblical history. They shared their adventure with their families, recounting every detail of the ark's construction, the great flood, and the miraculous survival of Noah's family and the animals.

Their families listened in amazement, and the children's excitement was contagious. They decided to create another journal entry, documenting their experiences with detailed drawings and descriptions. Each page captured a different aspect of their adventure, from the bustling construction site to the peaceful procession of animals into the ark. The children reflected on the lessons they had learned: the importance of faith and obedience, the value of hard work and perseverance, and the promise of God's protection and love. They felt a deep connection to Noah and his family, who had shown them what it meant to trust in God even in the face of great challenges.

As they settled back into their daily routines, the children knew that their time machine held many more adventures and that there were countless other stories to discover in the pages of the Bible. But for now, they were content with the memories of their journey with Noah, a journey that had taken them through the construction of the ark, the great flood, and the promise of a new beginning. They looked forward to the future with excitement, knowing that with each new adventure, they would learn more about God's plan for the world and their place in it. They were a team, a family, and nothing could stop them from exploring the wonders of the past and the lessons they held for the future. With their bond stronger than ever and their love for discovery unquenchable, they were ready to face the world together, one adventure at a time.

Chapter 3 - The Tower of Babel

James, Mary, David, and Linda couldn't wait to embark on their next adventure with the time machine. Their journeys to the creation of the world and Noah's Ark had been incredible, and they were eager to see what awaited them next. This time, they set the coordinates for the time of the Tower of Babel, curious to witness the events that led to the confusion of languages. With a hum and a flash, the time machine transported them to a bustling construction site in the ancient city of Babel. The children stepped out into a world filled with the sounds of hammering, sawing, and the shouts of workers. All around them, people were busy building a massive tower that stretched high into the sky. It was a sight to behold, a testament to human ambition and ingenuity. The children watched in awe as workers lifted huge stones and placed them meticulously into the growing structure.

As they wandered through the construction site, they noticed that everyone seemed to be speaking the same language. Communication was smooth and efficient, with no barriers or misunderstandings. The children marveled at how well everyone worked together, united by a common goal to build a tower that would reach the heavens. They overheard conversations about the purpose of the tower, and it became clear that the people of Babel were building it to make a name for themselves and to prevent being scattered across the earth. Their pride and ambition drove them to attempt something grand, something that would ensure their legacy.

The children continued to explore the site, observing the intricate designs and the sheer scale of the project. They could feel the determination and energy in the air, and they were impressed by the skill and coordination of the workers. But amidst the excitement, they couldn't shake the feeling that something was about to change. As they watched, a sudden shift seemed to ripple through the crowd. People who had been working side by side began to look at each other in confusion. The clear, harmonious language they had been speaking moments before started to sound like a jumble of incomprehensible sounds. The children realized they were witnessing the moment when God intervened to confuse the languages of the people.

Panic and frustration spread quickly through the workers. They shouted and gestured, trying to make themselves understood, but the more they tried, the more confusing and chaotic the scene became. Friends and coworkers who had communicated effortlessly before were now speaking different languages, unable to understand each other. The children could see the bewilderment and desperation on their faces as the realization dawned that their ambitious project had come to a grinding halt. The once-united workforce was now divided, unable to collaborate or continue building the tower. The children felt a mix of emotions as they observed the confusion and disarray. They felt sympathy for the workers, who had been so full of purpose and ambition, but they also understood the lesson that was being taught. The people's pride and desire to challenge God's authority had led to their downfall.

As the chaos continued, the children saw groups of people beginning to drift apart. Unable to communicate with one another, they started to gather with those who spoke the same language. Small clusters formed, each group speaking a different tongue, and they began to disperse in different directions. The great city of Babel, once a symbol of human unity and ambition, was now fracturing into smaller, isolated communities. The children watched as the tower, now abandoned and incomplete, stood as a stark reminder of the consequences of pride and disobedience. They felt a deep sense of humility as they realized the importance of respecting God's plan and recognizing the limits of human ambition.

As the sun set over the scattered groups of people, the children knew it was time to return home. They made their way back to the time machine, their hearts and minds full of the lessons they had learned.

With a final glance at the tower, they set the coordinates for home and stepped inside. The journey back felt reflective, and soon they were standing in their backyard once again. They shared their adventure with their families, recounting the incredible sights and the powerful lesson they had witnessed. Their families listened with rapt attention, amazed by the children's experiences. The children decided to document their journey in their journal, filling the pages with detailed drawings and descriptions of the Tower of Babel and the confusion of languages. Each page captured a different aspect of their adventure, from the bustling construction site to the chaotic moment when the languages were confused.

As they reflected on their journey, the children realized the importance of humility and the dangers of pride. They understood that unity and cooperation should be based on respect for God's will, rather than a desire to challenge it. Their adventure had taught them valuable lessons about the power of language and communication, and the need to remain humble and obedient to God's plan. They felt a deep connection to the story of Babel, and they knew that the lessons they had learned would stay with them for a lifetime. As they settled back into their daily routines, the children looked forward to their next adventure with the time machine. They knew there were countless other stories to discover in the pages of the Bible, each one filled with lessons and insights that would help them grow in their faith and understanding.

With each new journey, they felt their bond as friends growing stronger, and their love for discovery deepening. They were a team, a family, and nothing could stop them from exploring the wonders of the past and the lessons they held for the future. With their bond stronger than ever and their love for discovery unquenchable, they were ready to face the world together, one adventure at a time. They knew that their time machine held many more adventures, and they were eager to see where it would take them next. Whether they were witnessing the creation of the world, the construction of Noah's Ark, or the confusion of languages at Babel, each journey brought them closer to understanding God's plan and their place in it. They were excited to continue their travels through the pages of history, learning and growing with each new adventure.

Chapter 4 - God's Promise to Abraham

James, Mary, David, and Linda were eager for their next adventure with the time machine, having already witnessed the creation of the world, Noah's Ark, and the Tower of Babel. This time, they decided to travel to a pivotal moment in the history of faith: God's promise to Abraham. With a mix of excitement and anticipation, they set the coordinates and, within moments, found themselves in a vast, open landscape under a brilliant sky. They saw a group of tents clustered together, with flocks of sheep and goats grazing nearby. It was a scene of pastoral tranquility, but there was an air of anticipation as well. The children quickly spotted Abraham, a man of deep faith and wisdom, who was engaged in conversation with his wife, Sarah. Abraham's face radiated a sense of purpose and determination, and the children felt an instant connection to him. They approached the camp, and Abraham greeted them warmly, sensing that they were special visitors with a keen interest in his journey.

Abraham explained that God had called him to leave his homeland and journey to a land that He would show him, a land promised to his descendants. The children listened intently as Abraham recounted his initial call from God and the promises of blessings, numerous descendants, and a great nation. They could feel the weight of the promise and the faith it required to leave everything behind and trust in God's plan. The children accompanied Abraham as he journeyed through the land, experiencing the hardships and challenges of travel. They crossed arid deserts, climbed rocky hills, and traversed lush valleys, all the while observing Abraham's unwavering faith and commitment. They saw how he built altars to God at significant places, marking his gratitude and devotion.

One evening, as they sat around a campfire, Abraham shared the story of his nephew Lot and the difficult decision to part ways to avoid conflict between their herdsmen. The children admired Abraham's generosity and humility in allowing Lot to choose the fertile plains while he took the more challenging land. They understood that true faith often involves sacrifice and trust in God's provision. As they traveled further, the children witnessed God's covenant with Abraham. One night, God spoke to Abraham, promising that his descendants would be as numerous as the stars in the sky. The children looked up at the vast, twinkling expanse above and felt a sense of awe at the magnitude of the promise. They realized that God's plans were far greater than they could comprehend.

God instructed Abraham to prepare a covenant ceremony, and the children watched as Abraham obediently followed God's commands. He sacrificed animals and arranged the pieces, then waited for God's presence. As the sun set and darkness fell, a deep sleep overcame Abraham, and the children witnessed a vision of God's presence passing between the pieces, symbolizing His unbreakable promise. The solemnity and sacredness of the moment left a profound impact on the children, who understood that they were witnessing a divine agreement that would shape the course of history.

The journey continued, and the children observed the struggles and triumphs of Abraham's faith. They saw his moments of doubt and fear, such as when he and Sarah traveled to Egypt during a famine and faced the challenge of trusting God's protection. They also witnessed God's reassurance and continued blessings, such as the promise of a son despite Sarah's old age. One day, three visitors arrived at Abraham's tent, and the children sensed something extraordinary about them. Abraham welcomed the strangers with hospitality and respect, providing food and water for them. As they ate, one of the visitors revealed that Sarah would soon have a son. Sarah, listening from inside the tent, laughed in disbelief, but the visitor, who was God in human form, reaffirmed the promise.

The children were thrilled to witness the miraculous birth of Isaac, the long-awaited son of Abraham and Sarah. They saw the joy and fulfillment in Abraham's eyes as he held his newborn son, the tangible proof of God's faithfulness. They understood that God's promises might take time to unfold, but they were always fulfilled. The children also experienced the pain of Abraham's faith being tested when God asked him to sacrifice Isaac. They felt the tension and heartbreak as Abraham prepared to obey, believing that God could raise Isaac from the dead if necessary. At the last moment, an angel of the Lord intervened, and a ram was provided as a substitute sacrifice. The children breathed a sigh of relief, deeply moved by Abraham's unwavering faith and God's provision.

Throughout their journey, the children learned valuable lessons about faith, obedience, and trust in God's promises. They saw how Abraham's relationship with God was built on communication, trust, and unwavering commitment. They understood that faith was not just about believing but also about acting on that belief, even when the path was difficult or unclear. As their time with Abraham drew to a close, the children felt a deep sense of gratitude for the experiences and lessons they had gained. They said their goodbyes to Abraham and his family, feeling a strong bond with the patriarch of faith. They knew that their journey with Abraham had given them a deeper understanding of what it meant to live a life of faith and trust in God's promises.

Returning to the time machine, the children set the coordinates for home, reflecting on their incredible adventure. The journey back felt contemplative, and soon they were standing in their backyard once again. They shared their experiences with their families, recounting the lessons of faith, obedience, and trust they had learned from Abraham. Their families listened with awe and admiration, inspired by the children's stories. The children decided to document their journey in their journal, filling the pages with detailed drawings and descriptions of their time with Abraham. Each page captured a different aspect of their adventure, from the journey through the Promised Land to the covenant ceremony and the birth of Isaac.

As they reflected on their journey, the children realized the importance of holding on to faith and trusting in God's plan, even when it seemed impossible. They understood that God's promises were always fulfilled in His perfect timing. Their adventure with Abraham had taught them valuable lessons about perseverance, sacrifice, and the power of God's faithfulness. They felt a deep connection to the story of Abraham and knew that the lessons they had learned would stay with them for a lifetime. As they settled back into their daily routines, the children looked forward to their next adventure with the time machine. They knew there were countless other stories to discover in the pages of the Bible, each one filled with lessons and insights that would help them grow in their faith and understanding.

With each new journey, they felt their bond as friends growing stronger, and their love for discovery deepening. They were a team, a family, and nothing could stop them from exploring the wonders of the past and the lessons they held for the future. With their bond stronger than ever and their love for discovery unquenchable, they were ready to face the world together, one adventure at a time. They knew that their time machine held many more adventures, and they were eager to see where it would take them next. Whether they were witnessing the creation of the world, the construction of Noah's Ark, the confusion of languages at Babel, or the promises made to Abraham, each journey brought them closer to understanding God's plan and their place in it. They were excited to continue their travels through the pages of history, learning and growing with each new adventure.

Chapter 5 - Jacob's Dream at Bethel

James, Mary, David, and Linda had experienced incredible adventures with their time machine, journeying through pivotal moments in the Bible, and now they were ready for their next adventure. This time, they set the coordinates to witness Jacob's dream at Bethel, a moment of divine encounter that would shape Jacob's life and legacy. With the familiar hum of the time machine, they were transported back to a time of ancient wanderings, and they found themselves on a rugged path under a canopy of stars. The night was calm, and the air was filled with the sounds of crickets and the distant calls of night creatures. As they walked along the path, they saw a solitary figure ahead, traveling with nothing but a staff. It was Jacob, making his way to Haran to escape his brother Esau's wrath and to seek a wife among his mother's relatives.

The children approached Jacob, who welcomed them with a weary but kind smile. He explained that he was on a long journey, filled with uncertainty and fear, but he trusted in the God of his fathers, Abraham and Isaac. The children felt a deep connection to Jacob, understanding the weight of his journey and the hope he carried in his heart. As night fell, Jacob decided to rest. He found a smooth stone to use as a pillow and lay down to sleep. The children gathered around, curious and excited, knowing that something extraordinary was about to happen. They watched as Jacob drifted into a deep sleep, his face peaceful under the light of the moon.

Suddenly, the atmosphere around them changed. The night seemed to shimmer with a divine presence, and the children felt a sense of awe and reverence. They looked up and saw a magnificent ladder reaching from the earth to heaven. The ladder was made of light, and angels were ascending and descending on it. The sight was breathtaking, and the children could hardly believe their eyes. It was as if the heavens had opened, revealing a connection between God and man. At the top of the ladder stood the Lord, His presence radiating with glory and majesty. The children could feel His power and love, and they knew they were witnessing a holy moment.

The Lord spoke to Jacob, His voice filled with promise and assurance. "I am the Lord, the God of your father Abraham and the God of Isaac. I will give you and your descendants the land on which you are lying. Your descendants will be like the dust of the earth, and you will spread out to the west and to the east, to the north and to the south. All peoples on earth will be blessed through you and your offspring. I am with you and will watch over you wherever you go, and I will bring you back to this land. I will not leave you until I have done what I have promised you."

The children felt the weight of God's words and the magnitude of the promise He was making to Jacob. They understood that this was a covenant that would shape the destiny of Jacob's descendants and the future of God's people. As the vision continued, the children noticed the angels moving gracefully up and down the ladder, each one a messenger of God's will and purpose. They felt a sense of peace and protection, knowing that God was watching over Jacob and his journey. The vision faded, and the children watched as Jacob awoke with a start. He looked around, his eyes wide with wonder and awe. "Surely the Lord is in this place, and I was not aware of it," he said, his voice trembling with reverence. "How awesome is this place! This is none other than the house of God; this is the gate of heaven."

Jacob took the stone he had used as a pillow and set it up as a pillar, pouring oil on top of it to consecrate it. He named the place Bethel, which means "house of God." The children helped Jacob gather stones and build a small altar, feeling honored to participate in this act of worship and dedication. Jacob then made a vow, saying, "If God will be with me and will watch over me on this journey I am taking and will give me food to eat and clothes to wear so that I return safely to my father's household, then the Lord will be my God and this stone that I have set up as a pillar will be God's house, and of all that you give me I will give you a tenth."

The children were deeply moved by Jacob's faith and his commitment to honor God. They understood that this moment was a turning point in Jacob's life, a reaffirmation of God's promises and a declaration of his trust in God's provision and guidance. As the night turned to dawn, the children felt a sense of fulfillment and peace. They had witnessed a profound encounter between God and Jacob, one that would have lasting significance for generations to come. They knew that their adventure had given them a deeper understanding of God's faithfulness and the importance of trusting in His promises.

Reluctantly, they said their goodbyes to Jacob, who thanked them for their companionship and support. He continued on his journey with renewed strength and confidence, knowing that God was with him. The children made their way back to the time machine, their hearts full of the experiences and lessons they had gained. With a final glance at the stone pillar marking the place of Jacob's dream, they set the coordinates for home and stepped inside. The journey back felt reflective, and soon they were standing in their backyard once again. They shared their adventure with their families, recounting the awe-inspiring vision of the ladder to heaven and the powerful words of God's promise to Jacob. Their families listened with amazement, and the children's excitement was contagious.

They decided to document their journey in their journal, filling the pages with detailed drawings and descriptions of Jacob's dream and the angels ascending and descending the ladder. Each page captured a different aspect of their adventure, from the peaceful night under the stars to the divine encounter that reaffirmed God's covenant with Jacob. As they reflected on their journey, the children realized the importance of being aware of God's presence in their lives and trusting in His promises. They understood that, like Jacob, they were part of a greater story, one that was guided by God's love and faithfulness.

Their adventure had taught them valuable lessons about faith, trust, and the significance of divine encounters. They felt a deep connection to the story of Jacob and knew that the lessons they had learned would stay with them for a lifetime. As they settled back into their daily routines, the children looked forward to their next adventure with the time machine. They knew there were countless other stories to discover in the pages of the Bible, each one filled with lessons and insights that would help them grow in their faith and understanding.

With each new journey, they felt their bond as friends growing stronger, and their love for discovery deepening. They were a team, a family, and nothing could stop them from exploring the wonders of the past and the lessons they held for the future. With their bond stronger than ever and their love for discovery unquenchable, they were ready to face the world together, one adventure at a time. They knew that their time machine held many more adventures, and they were eager to see where it would take them next. Whether they were witnessing the creation of the world, the construction of Noah's Ark, the confusion of languages at Babel, God's promises to Abraham, or Jacob's divine dream at Bethel, each journey brought them closer to understanding God's plan and their place in it. They were excited to continue their travels through the pages of history, learning and growing with each new adventure, and they were confident that their time machine would guide them to even more incredible experiences in the future.

Chapter 6 - Joseph's Dreams and Betrayal

James, Mary, David, and Linda were thrilled to embark on another adventure with their time machine, eager to explore the story of Joseph and his colorful coat. Setting the coordinates, they felt the familiar hum and, in a flash, were transported back to ancient Canaan. They found themselves amidst the sprawling fields and flocks of a large, prosperous family. As they approached, they saw a young man, Joseph, standing out among his brothers with a vibrant, multi-colored coat that shimmered in the sunlight. Joseph greeted them warmly, his eyes sparkling with the dreams and ambitions of youth. He was excited to share his story and show them the beautiful coat his father, Jacob, had given him as a symbol of his special love. The children admired the intricate design and rich colors of the coat, sensing the deep bond between Joseph and his father. However, they also noticed the dark glances and murmurs of jealousy from his brothers.

As they spent more time with Joseph, the children learned about his extraordinary dreams. Joseph recounted a recent dream in which he and his brothers were binding sheaves of grain in the field, and his sheaf stood upright while his brothers' sheaves gathered around and bowed down to it. He also shared another dream in which the sun, moon, and eleven stars bowed down to him. While the children found the dreams fascinating and symbolic, they saw that Joseph's brothers were not pleased. The dreams seemed to fuel their jealousy and resentment, making them feel threatened by the idea that Joseph might one day rule over them. The children sensed that something ominous was brewing.

One day, Jacob sent Joseph to check on his brothers, who were grazing their flocks near Shechem. The children decided to accompany Joseph on this journey, eager to support their new friend. As they approached, they saw Joseph's brothers plotting against him. The brothers, filled with jealousy and anger, seized Joseph and stripped him of his colorful coat. They threw him into a dry cistern, leaving him trapped and helpless. The children watched in horror, feeling the intensity of Joseph's betrayal and the coldness of his brothers' actions. Joseph's pleas for mercy echoed in their ears as they witnessed the brothers' next move. They saw a caravan of Ishmaelite traders approaching, and Joseph's brothers decided to sell him into slavery. They pulled Joseph out of the cistern and handed him over to the traders for twenty pieces of silver. The children's hearts ached as they saw Joseph being led away in chains, his dreams shattered and his future uncertain.

The brothers then concocted a cruel lie to cover up their betrayal. They dipped Joseph's colorful coat in goat's blood and took it back to their father, Jacob, implying that Joseph had been killed by a wild animal. The children watched as Jacob, heartbroken and devastated, mourned the loss of his beloved son. The sight of Jacob's grief was almost too much to bear, and the children felt a deep sense of sadness and injustice. Despite the pain and betrayal, the children sensed that this was not the end of Joseph's story. They knew from their studies that Joseph's journey was far from over and that there were greater plans in store for him. They felt a spark of hope amidst the sorrow, knowing that Joseph's faith and resilience would see him through.

As the time machine signaled it was time to return home, the children said their goodbyes to Joseph, promising to carry his story with them and to remember the lessons they had learned. With heavy hearts, they stepped back into the time machine and set the coordinates for home. The journey back felt somber, and soon they were standing in their backyard once again. They shared their adventure with their families, recounting the betrayal and the incredible resilience of Joseph. Their families listened with a mix of sadness and admiration, understanding the gravity of the events the children had witnessed. The children decided to document their journey in their journal, filling the pages with detailed drawings and descriptions of Joseph's colorful coat, his dreams, and the betrayal by his brothers. Each page captured a different aspect of their adventure, from the beauty of the coat to the sorrow of Joseph's enslavement.

As they reflected on their journey, the children realized the importance of resilience and faith in the face of adversity. They understood that Joseph's dreams, though temporarily shattered, were part of a larger plan that would unfold in time. Their adventure had taught them valuable lessons about jealousy, betrayal, and the strength to overcome even the darkest of circumstances. They felt a deep connection to Joseph's story and knew that the lessons they had learned would stay with them for a lifetime. As they settled back into their daily routines, the children looked forward to their next adventure with the time machine. They knew there were countless other stories to discover in the pages of the Bible, each one filled with lessons and insights that would help them grow in their faith and understanding.

With each new journey, they felt their bond as friends growing stronger, and their love for discovery deepening. They were a team, a family, and nothing could stop them from exploring the wonders of the past and the lessons they held for the future. With their bond stronger than ever and their love for discovery unquenchable, they were ready to face the world together, one adventure at a time. They knew that their time machine held many more adventures, and they were eager to see where it would take them next. Whether they were witnessing the creation of the world, the construction of Noah's Ark, the confusion of languages at Babel, God's promises to Abraham, Jacob's divine dream at Bethel, or Joseph's dreams and betrayal, each journey brought them closer to understanding God's plan and their place in it. They were excited to continue their travels through the pages of history, learning and growing with each new adventure, and they were confident that their time machine would guide them to even more incredible experiences in the future.

Chapter 7 - Joseph's Rise to Power

James, Mary, David, and Linda were excited for their next adventure, curious to see how the story of Joseph would unfold after witnessing his betrayal by his brothers. Setting the coordinates, they activated the time machine and were transported to ancient Egypt, arriving in a bustling city filled with grandeur and activity. They found themselves in the presence of a confident and composed Joseph, now a young man with an air of wisdom and authority. Joseph greeted them warmly, and the children were eager to hear how he had gone from a slave to a respected figure in Pharaoh's court. Joseph began to recount his incredible journey, explaining how he had been sold into slavery and ended up in the house of Potiphar, an officer of Pharaoh. Despite the challenges he faced, Joseph's faith and integrity earned him Potiphar's trust, and he was put in charge of the household. However, false accusations by Potiphar's wife led to his imprisonment. The children listened intently, marveling at Joseph's resilience and unwavering faith in God.

Joseph described his time in prison, where he continued to find favor and was put in charge of the other prisoners. It was there that he interpreted the dreams of Pharaoh's cupbearer and baker, accurately predicting their fates. The children could sense that these moments were pivotal in Joseph's journey, demonstrating his God-given gift of interpreting dreams. Two years later, Pharaoh himself had two troubling dreams that none of his wise men or magicians could interpret. The children watched in awe as Joseph, summoned from prison, stood before Pharaoh with confidence and humility. Joseph listened to Pharaoh's dreams: in one, seven healthy cows were devoured by seven gaunt cows, and in the other, seven full heads of grain were swallowed by seven thin, scorched heads of grain. Joseph explained that the dreams were a warning from God, foretelling seven years of abundance followed by seven years of severe famine.

The children were captivated by Joseph's wisdom and composure as he provided a solution to Pharaoh's dilemma. He proposed appointing a discerning and wise man to oversee the land of Egypt, storing surplus grain during the years of abundance to prepare for the famine. Pharaoh was impressed by Joseph's insight and recognized the presence of God in him. With a sense of destiny, Pharaoh appointed Joseph as the second-in-command of Egypt, giving him authority over the land and the task of preparing for the impending famine. The children watched as Joseph was robed in fine linen, adorned with a gold chain, and given Pharaoh's signet ring, symbolizing his new position of power and trust. They felt a sense of triumph and validation for Joseph, who had endured so much hardship yet remained faithful to God.

As Joseph set about his new responsibilities, the children observed the meticulous planning and organization he implemented. He traveled throughout Egypt, overseeing the collection of grain and ensuring the storehouses were filled. His leadership and foresight earned him the respect and admiration of the Egyptian people. The children were amazed by Joseph's ability to transform adversity into opportunity, guided by his faith and wisdom. During this time, Joseph married Asenath, the daughter of Potiphera, priest of On, and they had two sons, Manasseh and Ephraim. The children saw the joy and fulfillment in Joseph's life, as he embraced his new family and responsibilities with gratitude and humility. He named his sons to reflect his journey: Manasseh, meaning "God has made me forget all my trouble and my father's household," and Ephraim, meaning "God has made me fruitful in the land of my suffering."

As the years of abundance passed, the children witnessed the arrival of the years of famine. The severity of the famine affected not only Egypt but also the surrounding nations. People from all over came to Egypt to buy grain, as Joseph had prepared for such a time. The children saw how Joseph's careful planning and management saved countless lives and ensured the prosperity of Egypt during the difficult years. One day, as they were observing Joseph at work, the children saw a familiar group of men approach, seeking to buy grain. They were Joseph's brothers, who had come to Egypt out of desperation, unaware that the powerful official they were dealing with was the brother they had betrayed years earlier. The children could feel the tension and emotion as Joseph recognized his brothers but chose to conceal his identity.

Joseph tested his brothers, accusing them of being spies and imprisoning them for three days. He then released them, keeping Simeon as a hostage, and sent the others back to Canaan with grain, instructing them to return with their youngest brother, Benjamin. The children sensed that Joseph was trying to discern if his brothers had changed and if they regretted their actions. As time passed, the brothers returned to Egypt with Benjamin, and the children observed Joseph's internal struggle between revealing his identity and continuing the test. Joseph arranged a feast for his brothers, showing special favor to Benjamin, and then planted his silver cup in Benjamin's sack as they departed. When the cup was discovered, the brothers were brought back to Joseph, fearing for their lives.

Joseph finally revealed his identity to his brothers in an emotional and tearful moment. He reassured them, saying, "I am Joseph! Is my father still living?" His brothers were stunned and terrified, but Joseph comforted them, explaining that it was God's plan for him to be in Egypt to save lives during the famine. The children were deeply moved by Joseph's forgiveness and the reconciliation that followed. Joseph sent his brothers back to Canaan to bring their father, Jacob, and their entire family to Egypt. The children watched as the brothers returned with the joyful news and saw Jacob's overwhelming happiness at learning his beloved son was alive. Jacob and his family journeyed to Egypt, where they were warmly welcomed by Joseph and settled in the land of Goshen.

The children felt a sense of fulfillment and closure as they witnessed the reunion of Joseph and his family. They marveled at how God had orchestrated Joseph's journey from betrayal to triumph, using every hardship to prepare him for a greater purpose. They understood that Joseph's rise to power was not just a story of personal success but a testament to faith, resilience, and the divine plan that had guided his life. As their time in ancient Egypt drew to a close, the children said their goodbyes to Joseph and his family, feeling honored to have been part of such a remarkable story. They returned to the time machine, their hearts and minds full of the experiences and lessons they had gained. With a final glance at the bustling city of Egypt, they set the coordinates for home and stepped inside.

The journey back felt reflective, and soon they were standing in their backyard once again. They shared their adventure with their families, recounting Joseph's rise to power and the incredible journey that had led him to become a savior for many. Their families listened with awe and admiration, inspired by the children's stories. The children decided to document their journey in their journal, filling the pages with detailed drawings and descriptions of Joseph's dreams, his betrayal, his rise to power, and the reconciliation with his brothers. Each page captured a different aspect of their adventure, from the grandeur of Pharaoh's court to the emotional reunion with Jacob.

As they reflected on their journey, the children realized the importance of faith, resilience, and forgiveness. They understood that Joseph's story was a powerful example of how God's plans can turn even the darkest moments into opportunities for growth and redemption. Their adventure had taught them valuable lessons about perseverance, trust, and the power of reconciliation. They felt a deep connection to Joseph's story and knew that the lessons they had learned would stay with them for a lifetime. As they settled back into their daily routines, the children looked forward to their next adventure with the time machine. They knew there were countless other stories to discover in the pages of the Bible, each one filled with lessons and insights that would help them grow in their faith and understanding.

With each new journey, they felt their bond as friends growing stronger, and their love for discovery deepening. They were a team, a family, and nothing could stop them from exploring the wonders of the past and the lessons they held for the future. With their bond stronger than ever and their love for discovery unquenchable, they were ready to face the world together, one adventure at a time. They knew that their time machine held many more adventures, and they were eager to see where it would take them next. Whether they were witnessing the creation of the world, the construction of Noah's Ark, the confusion of languages at Babel, God's promises to Abraham, Jacob's divine dream at Bethel, Joseph's dreams and betrayal, or his rise to power, each journey brought them closer to understanding God's plan and their place in it. They were excited to continue their travels through the pages of history, learning and growing with each new adventure, and they were confident that their time machine would guide them to even more incredible experiences in the future.

Chapter 8 - The Birth of Moses

James, Mary, David, and Linda were ready for another thrilling adventure, this time to witness the birth of Moses. They set the coordinates on their time machine and, with a familiar hum and flash, were transported back to ancient Egypt, a land filled with towering pyramids, lush riverbanks, and the bustling activity of a thriving civilization. They found themselves in a quiet, modest home of an Israelite family, where they were greeted by a kind woman named Jochebed, who welcomed them with a warm smile despite the fear in her eyes. The children quickly realized they were in the home of Moses' parents, who were living under the cruel decree of Pharaoh that all Hebrew baby boys must be killed.

Jochebed explained to the children that she had given birth to a beautiful baby boy and had managed to keep him hidden for three months. As she spoke, she gently rocked the infant Moses, who gazed up at her with trusting eyes. The children could sense the love and desperation in Jochebed's actions as she tried to protect her son from the dangers that lurked outside their door. They watched in awe as Jochebed and her husband, Amram, devised a daring plan to save their baby. They carefully crafted a small basket out of papyrus reeds, waterproofing it with tar and pitch to ensure it would float. The children helped gather the materials and watched as the basket took shape, their hearts pounding with a mix of fear and hope.

One early morning, Jochebed placed the sleeping baby Moses into the basket, her eyes filled with tears and determination. The children accompanied her and her daughter Miriam to the edge of the Nile River, where the reeds grew thick and tall. With a final kiss and a prayer, Jochebed placed the basket among the reeds, entrusting her precious son to the waters of the Nile and the hands of God. The children stayed hidden with Miriam, their hearts aching as they watched the basket gently float away. They marveled at Miriam's bravery as she stood watch, keeping an eye on her brother's journey down the river. The Nile was both beautiful and intimidating, its waters teeming with life and mystery.

As the basket drifted downstream, the children followed at a safe distance, their eyes never leaving the tiny vessel. They saw the basket come to rest near the royal palace, where Pharaoh's daughter, Princess Hatshepsut, had come to bathe with her attendants. The princess noticed the basket and instructed her maidservants to retrieve it. The children held their breath as the basket was brought to the shore and opened. The princess gasped in surprise and delight at the sight of the beautiful baby boy inside. Moses cried out, and the princess's heart melted with compassion. She recognized the child as one of the Hebrew babies, yet she felt an overwhelming urge to protect him. The children watched in awe as the princess decided to adopt the baby as her own, naming him Moses, meaning "drawn out of the water."

Miriam, who had been watching from a distance, bravely approached the princess and offered to find a Hebrew woman to nurse the baby. The princess agreed, and Miriam quickly ran to fetch her mother, Jochebed. The children could hardly contain their excitement as they saw Jochebed's joy and relief at being reunited with her son, even if it was only for a little while. Jochebed was brought to the palace, where she was tasked with nursing and caring for Moses until he was old enough to be brought to the princess. The children were filled with admiration for Jochebed's strength and faith, knowing that she had saved her son and ensured his future, even if it meant letting him go.

As time passed, the children watched Moses grow under the loving care of his mother and the protection of the princess. They saw the bond that formed between Moses and his adoptive mother, as well as the influence of his Hebrew heritage. Moses learned about the God of his ancestors, the struggles of his people, and the culture of the Egyptians, preparing him for the incredible journey that lay ahead. When the time came for Moses to be brought to the palace, the children felt a mix of sadness and excitement. They knew that this was just the beginning of Moses' extraordinary life, a life that would lead him to become one of the greatest leaders and prophets in history. They accompanied Moses to the palace, where he was welcomed with open arms by the princess, who had come to love him as her own son.

The children observed the opulence and grandeur of the royal palace, a stark contrast to the humble home where Moses had been born. They saw Moses adapt to his new life, learning the ways of the Egyptian court while never forgetting his true heritage. They admired his resilience and strength, qualities that would serve him well in the years to come. As their time in ancient Egypt drew to a close, the children felt a deep sense of awe and inspiration. They had witnessed the beginning of an incredible journey, one that would change the course of history and fulfill God's promise to deliver His people from bondage. They said their goodbyes to Moses and his family, feeling grateful for the experiences and lessons they had gained.

Returning to the time machine, the children set the coordinates for home, reflecting on their incredible adventure. The journey back felt contemplative, and soon they were standing in their backyard once again. They shared their adventure with their families, recounting the miraculous story of baby Moses, his rescue from the Nile, and his adoption by Pharaoh's daughter. Their families listened with awe and admiration, inspired by the children's stories. The children decided to document their journey in their journal, filling the pages with detailed drawings and descriptions of Moses' early life, the basket in the Nile, and his adoption by the princess. Each page captured a different aspect of their adventure, from the humble home of Jochebed to the grandeur of the royal palace.

As they reflected on their journey, the children realized the importance of faith, courage, and the providence of God. They understood that Moses' story was a powerful example of how God's plans can unfold in the most unexpected ways, turning seemingly hopeless situations into opportunities for deliverance and redemption. Their adventure had taught them valuable lessons about trust, resilience, and the power of divine intervention. They felt a deep connection to Moses' story and knew that the lessons they had learned would stay with them for a lifetime. As they settled back into their daily routines, the children looked forward to their next adventure with the time machine. They knew there were countless other stories to discover in the pages of the Bible, each one filled with lessons and insights that would help them grow in their faith and understanding.

With each new journey, they felt their bond as friends growing stronger, and their love for discovery deepening. They were a team, a family, and nothing could stop them from exploring the wonders of the past and the lessons they held for the future. With their bond stronger than ever and their love for discovery unquenchable, they were ready to face the world together, one adventure at a time. They knew that their time machine held many more adventures, and they were eager to see where it would take them next. Whether they were witnessing the creation of the world, the construction of Noah's Ark, the confusion of languages at Babel, God's promises to Abraham, Jacob's divine dream at Bethel, Joseph's dreams and betrayal, his rise to power, or the birth of Moses, each journey brought them closer to understanding God's plan and their place in it. They were excited to continue their travels through the pages of history, learning and growing with each new adventure, and they were confident that their time machine would guide them to even more incredible experiences in the future.

Chapter 9 - Moses and the Burning Bush

James, Mary, David, and Linda, full of curiosity and excitement, gathered around the time machine for another adventure. They had witnessed the early life of Moses and now set their coordinates to experience one of the most profound moments in biblical history: Moses' encounter with God at the burning bush. With a familiar hum and flash, they found themselves transported to a desolate, rugged landscape, the vast wilderness of Midian. The children spotted Moses, now a shepherd, tending his father-in-law Jethro's flock. Moses appeared older and more contemplative, his life as a prince of Egypt a distant memory. The children approached him with a mix of reverence and eagerness, sensing that something extraordinary was about to happen.

As they walked with Moses, the children noticed a peculiar sight in the distance—a bush that seemed to be engulfed in flames but was not consumed by the fire. Moses, curious and drawn to the strange phenomenon, decided to investigate, and the children followed closely behind. The closer they got, the more they could feel an aura of holiness surrounding the area. When Moses reached the burning bush, he was awestruck by its brilliance and the fact that it remained unburned. Suddenly, a voice called out to him from the bush, "Moses, Moses!" Trembling with fear and wonder, Moses replied, "Here I am." The children watched in silent awe as the voice continued, "Do not come any closer. Take off your sandals, for the place where you are standing is holy ground."

Moses obeyed, removing his sandals and bowing low to the ground. The children, feeling the sacredness of the moment, did the same, their hearts pounding with anticipation. The voice from the bush then revealed itself, "I am the God of your father, the God of Abraham, the God of Isaac, and the God of Jacob." Moses hid his face, afraid to look at God, and the children felt a deep sense of reverence and humility.

God continued to speak, explaining that He had seen the misery of His people in Egypt and had heard their cries for deliverance. The children's hearts ached as they thought of the suffering of the Israelites, and they understood the significance of this divine encounter. God declared that He had come down to rescue His people from the hand of the Egyptians and to bring them to a land flowing with milk and honey.

The children watched as Moses listened intently, his face reflecting a mix of awe and confusion. God then revealed His plan, saying, "So now, go. I am sending you to Pharaoh to bring My people the Israelites out of Egypt." Moses was stunned and overwhelmed by the magnitude of the task before him. The children could see the doubt and fear in his eyes as he questioned his own ability to carry out such a monumental mission. "Who am I that I should go to Pharaoh and bring the Israelites out of Egypt?" Moses asked, his voice trembling. God reassured him, "I will be with you. And this will be the sign to you that it is I who have sent you: when you have brought the people out of Egypt, you will worship God on this mountain."

Despite the reassurance, Moses continued to express his concerns, wondering what he should say if the Israelites asked for the name of the God who sent him. The children leaned in, eager to hear God's response. God said to Moses, "I AM WHO I AM. This is what you are to say to the Israelites: 'I AM has sent me to you.'" The children felt the power and mystery of God's name, understanding that it encompassed His eternal and self-existent nature. God then provided further instructions, telling Moses to gather the elders of Israel and convey His message of deliverance. He also warned that Pharaoh would not easily let the Israelites go, but that He would perform mighty wonders to compel him.

The children watched as Moses continued to express his doubts, worried about his own inadequacies and lack of eloquence. "Pardon your servant, Lord, but I have never been eloquent, neither in the past nor since you have spoken to your servant. I am slow of speech and tongue," Moses pleaded. God responded with patience and assurance, "Who gave human beings their mouths? Who makes them deaf or mute? Who gives them sight or makes them blind? Is it not I, the Lord? Now go; I will help you speak and will teach you what to say." Despite God's assurances, Moses still felt overwhelmed and asked God to send someone else. The children felt a mix of empathy and frustration, understanding Moses' fear but also recognizing the importance of his calling. God, in His infinite wisdom, agreed to send Aaron, Moses' brother, to assist him. Aaron would speak to the people on Moses' behalf, and together they would lead the Israelites out of Egypt.

With the divine encounter coming to a close, the children felt the weight of the mission ahead of Moses. They had witnessed a profound moment of divine communication, one that would set into motion the liberation of an entire nation. They admired Moses' honesty in expressing his fears and doubts, and they were inspired by God's unwavering support and guidance. As they prepared to return home, the children said their goodbyes to Moses, who was now filled with a sense of purpose and determination. They knew that Moses' journey was just beginning and that he would face many challenges, but they also knew that he was not alone—God was with him every step of the way.

Returning to the time machine, the children set the coordinates for home, reflecting on their incredible adventure. The journey back felt contemplative, and soon they were standing in their backyard once again. They shared their experience with their families, recounting the awe-inspiring encounter at the burning bush and the powerful call that Moses had received. Their families listened with awe and admiration, inspired by the children's stories. The children decided to document their journey in their journal, filling the pages with detailed drawings and descriptions of the burning bush, the sacred ground, and God's call to Moses. Each page captured a different aspect of their adventure, from the rugged wilderness of Midian to the divine encounter that would change the course of history.

As they reflected on their journey, the children realized the importance of faith, courage, and obedience. They understood that Moses' story was a powerful example of how God calls and equips those He chooses, even when they feel inadequate or unworthy. Their adventure had taught them valuable lessons about trust, humility, and the power of divine intervention. They felt a deep connection to Moses' story and knew that the lessons they had learned would stay with them for a lifetime. As they settled back into their daily routines, the children looked forward to their next adventure with the time machine. They knew there were countless other stories to discover in the pages of the Bible, each one filled with lessons and insights that would help them grow in their faith and understanding.

With each new journey, they felt their bond as friends growing stronger, and their love for discovery deepening. They were a team, a family, and nothing could stop them from exploring the wonders of the past and the lessons they held for the future. With their bond stronger than ever and their love for discovery unquenchable, they were ready to face the world together, one adventure at a time. They knew that their time machine held many more adventures, and they were eager to see where it would take them next. Whether they were witnessing the creation of the world, the construction of Noah's Ark, the confusion of languages at Babel, God's promises to Abraham, Jacob's divine dream at Bethel, Joseph's dreams and betrayal, his rise to power, the birth of Moses, or his encounter with God at the burning bush, each journey brought them closer to understanding God's plan and their place in it. They were excited to continue their travels through the pages of history, learning and growing with each new adventure, and they were confident that their time machine would guide them to even more incredible experiences in the future.

Chapter 10 - The Ten Plagues of Egypt

James, Mary, David, and Linda were brimming with excitement as they gathered around the time machine, ready for their next adventure. This time, they set the coordinates to witness the Ten Plagues of Egypt and the liberation of the Israelites. With a familiar hum and flash, they were transported back to ancient Egypt, arriving in a land on the brink of a divine showdown. They found themselves in the heart of Pharaoh's palace, where Moses and Aaron stood before the proud and defiant ruler. Pharaoh, with his ornate headdress and regal robes, refused to listen to their plea to let the Israelites go. The children felt the tension in the room, understanding that they were about to witness the unfolding of God's mighty hand.

The first plague began as Aaron struck the Nile River with his staff, and the water turned into blood. The children watched in amazement and horror as the once life-giving river became a source of death and stench. Fish floated lifelessly to the surface, and the Egyptians were left scrambling to find drinkable water. Despite this terrifying sign, Pharaoh's heart remained hardened, and he refused to let the Israelites go. The children followed Moses and Aaron as they confronted Pharaoh again, bringing the second plague: frogs. Frogs swarmed the land, invading homes, beds, and kitchens. The children could hear the incessant croaking and saw the frustration and panic on the faces of the Egyptians. Yet, even as Pharaoh begged for relief and Moses prayed for the frogs to depart, Pharaoh's heart hardened once more when the plague ended.

Next came the plague of gnats. Aaron struck the dust of the ground, and it turned into gnats that tormented people and animals alike. The children watched as the tiny insects covered everything, causing misery and discomfort. The Egyptian magicians attempted to replicate this miracle but failed, admitting that it was the finger of God. Still, Pharaoh's heart remained unmoved. The fourth plague brought swarms of flies, filling the air and infesting the land of Egypt, yet sparing the land of Goshen where the Israelites lived. The children observed the clear distinction between the afflicted Egyptians and the protected Israelites, a powerful sign of God's favor and protection over His people. Pharaoh, desperate for relief, promised to let the Israelites go but once the flies were gone, he reneged on his promise.

The fifth plague struck the livestock of Egypt, killing horses, donkeys, camels, cattle, sheep, and goats. The children saw the devastation in the fields, with dead animals lying in heaps, yet not a single animal belonging to the Israelites was harmed. Despite the economic and emotional toll, Pharaoh's heart remained stubborn. The sixth plague brought painful boils that afflicted both people and animals. The children watched in sympathy as the Egyptians suffered from the painful sores, their cries of anguish filling the air. The magicians, who could no longer stand before Moses and Aaron because of the boils, admitted defeat, but Pharaoh's heart remained unyielding.

The seventh plague was a storm of hail, mingled with fire, that struck down everything in its path—humans, animals, and crops. The children witnessed the terrifying power of the storm, the sky darkening as hailstones and lightning wreaked havoc on the land. Those who heeded Moses' warning and sheltered their servants and animals were spared, but many Egyptians suffered great loss. Pharaoh, seeing the destruction, admitted his sin and promised to let the Israelites go. However, once the storm ceased, his heart hardened again.

The eighth plague brought locusts that devoured everything the hail had left behind. The children saw the land stripped bare, the once fertile fields now barren and desolate. Pharaoh's officials pleaded with him to let the Israelites go, warning of Egypt's impending ruin, but Pharaoh's heart remained hardened. The ninth plague brought three days of darkness over Egypt, a darkness so thick it could be felt. The children experienced the eerie stillness and fear that gripped the

Egyptians, while the Israelites had light in their dwellings. Despite this overwhelming sign, Pharaoh remained obstinate.

Finally, the tenth plague was announced: the death of the firstborn. The children felt the gravity of this final judgment as Moses instructed the Israelites to sacrifice a lamb and mark their doorposts with its blood, so the angel of death would pass over their homes. The children observed the Israelites' solemn preparations, sensing their fear and hope. That night, they heard the cries of the Egyptians as the firstborn in every household, from Pharaoh's palace to the humblest servant, were struck down. The children's hearts ached for the grieving families, but they also understood the fulfillment of God's warning to Pharaoh.

In the aftermath of this devastating plague, Pharaoh finally relented, summoning Moses and Aaron in the middle of the night. "Go," he said, "worship the Lord as you have requested. Take your flocks and herds, and leave. And also bless me." The children felt a surge of relief and triumph as they witnessed the Israelites' liberation. They followed the Israelites as they hastily gathered their belongings, their hearts filled with hope and anticipation. They saw the people of Egypt, eager to see the Israelites depart, giving them silver, gold, and clothing.

The journey out of Egypt began, and the children walked alongside the Israelites, feeling the collective excitement and nervousness of the crowd. They saw the hand of God guiding and protecting His people as a pillar of cloud by day and a pillar of fire by night led them on their way. As they reached the shores of the Red Sea, the children felt the tension rise once again. Pharaoh, in a final act of defiance, had sent his army to pursue the Israelites, trapping them between the sea and the advancing Egyptians. The children could see the fear in the eyes of the Israelites as they cried out to Moses.

Moses, with unwavering faith, stretched out his hand over the sea, and the children watched in awe as the waters parted, creating a dry path through the sea. The Israelites began to cross, the walls of water towering on either side. The children felt the wind on their faces and the sense of divine protection as they hurried along the path. As the last of the Israelites reached the other side, the Egyptian army charged into the sea after them. Moses stretched out his hand once more, and the waters returned, drowning the entire army. The children stood with the Israelites on the far shore, witnessing the complete and utter defeat of their pursuers.

The children felt a surge of joy and gratitude as they saw the Israelites celebrating their miraculous deliverance. They sang songs of praise and danced, giving thanks to God for His mighty acts. The children joined in the celebration, their hearts full of the wonder and power they had witnessed. They understood that they had been part of a pivotal moment in history, a story of liberation and faith that would be told for generations to come.

As the time machine signaled it was time to return home, the children said their goodbyes to the Israelites, feeling honored to have been part of their incredible journey. They returned to the time machine, their hearts and minds full of the experiences and lessons they had gained. With a final glance at the joyous scene before them, they set the coordinates for home and stepped inside.

The journey back felt reflective, and soon they were standing in their backyard once again. They shared their adventure with their families, recounting the awe-inspiring plagues and the miraculous deliverance of the Israelites. Their families listened with awe and admiration, inspired by the children's stories. The children decided to document their journey in their journal, filling the pages with detailed drawings and descriptions of each plague, the parting of the Red Sea, and the celebration of the Israelites' liberation. Each page captured a different aspect of their adventure, from the devastation of the plagues to the joy of freedom.

As they reflected on their journey, the children realized the importance of faith, resilience, and the power of divine intervention. They understood that the story of the Ten Plagues and the liberation of the Israelites was a powerful testament to God's justice, mercy, and unwavering commitment to His people. Their adventure had taught them valuable lessons about trust, perseverance, and the significance of freedom. They felt a deep connection to the story of Moses and the Israelites and knew that the lessons they had learned would stay with them for a lifetime.

As they settled back into their daily routines, the children looked forward to their next adventure with the time machine. They knew there were countless other stories to discover in the pages of the Bible, each one filled with lessons and insights that would help them grow in their faith and understanding. With each new journey, they felt their bond as friends growing stronger, and their love for discovery deepening. They were a team, a family, and nothing could stop them from exploring the wonders of the past and the lessons they held for the future.

With their bond stronger than ever and their love for discovery unquenchable, they were ready to face the world together, one adventure at a time. They knew that their time machine held many more adventures, and they were eager to see where it would take them next. Whether they were witnessing the creation of the world, the construction of Noah's Ark, the confusion of languages at Babel, God's promises to Abraham, Jacob's divine dream at Bethel, Joseph's dreams and betrayal, his rise to power, the birth of Moses, his encounter with God at the burning bush, or the Ten Plagues of Egypt, each journey brought them closer to understanding God's plan and their place in it. They were excited to continue their travels through the pages of history, learning and growing with each new adventure, and they were confident that their time machine would guide them to even more incredible experiences in the future.

Chapter 11 - Parting of the Red Sea

James, Mary, David, and Linda, buzzing with anticipation for their next adventure, gathered around the time machine and set the coordinates to witness the miraculous parting of the Red Sea. With a familiar hum and flash, they were transported to the edge of the Red Sea, standing amidst a multitude of Israelites who were fleeing from their bondage in Egypt. The children saw the fear and desperation on the faces of the people as they looked back at the approaching Egyptian army, the sound of chariots and horses growing louder by the moment. Moses, the leader of the Israelites, stood at the front, his face a mixture of determination and faith. The children felt the tension in the air as the people cried out to Moses, questioning why they had been led out of Egypt only to face certain death at the hands of Pharaoh's soldiers. Moses, with unwavering confidence, reassured them to not be afraid and to stand firm, for they would see the deliverance the Lord would bring them that day.

The children watched in awe as Moses stretched out his hand over the sea, holding the staff that had performed so many miracles. Suddenly, a powerful east wind began to blow, and the waters of the Red Sea started to part. The children's eyes widened in amazement as the waters formed towering walls on either side, creating a dry path through the sea. The Israelites, their fear turning to hope, began to move forward, stepping cautiously onto the dry seabed. The children followed, feeling the rush of the wind and the spray of the sea as they walked between the walls of water. It was a surreal and awe-inspiring sight, the sea transformed into a pathway of deliverance.

As they moved forward, the children saw families clinging to each other, their faces a mix of relief and urgency. They helped guide the elderly and the young, ensuring that everyone made it safely through the miraculous passage. The sense of community and shared purpose was palpable, each step taking them further from their past of oppression and closer to freedom. The sound of the Egyptian army's pursuit grew louder, and the children's hearts raced with the urgency of the moment. They looked back and saw Pharaoh's chariots entering the pathway, determined to recapture the fleeing Israelites. The children felt the tension rise once more as they neared the far shore, urging everyone to move faster.

Moses stood at the edge of the sea, watching as the last of the Israelites crossed to safety. With a commanding presence, he once again stretched out his hand over the sea. The children felt a surge of anticipation as the walls of water began to collapse, crashing down with a tremendous roar. The Egyptian army, caught in the midst of the sea, was engulfed by the returning waters. The children watched as the sea swallowed the chariots and horses, the sound of victory mingling with the cries of the Egyptians. Relief and joy swept over the Israelites as they realized they were finally free from their pursuers. The children joined in the jubilant celebration, their hearts swelling with gratitude and awe at the miraculous deliverance they had witnessed.

The Israelites gathered on the shore, and the children stood with them, feeling the weight of the moment. Moses, with a look of profound reverence, led the people in a song of praise to the Lord. The children listened as the words echoed across the waters, a testament to the power and faithfulness of God. "I will sing to the Lord, for he is highly exalted. Both horse and driver he has hurled into the sea. The Lord is my strength and my defense; he has become my salvation. He is my God, and I will praise him, my father's God, and I will exalt him." The children felt a deep connection to the words, understanding the profound significance of the deliverance they had just witnessed.

As the celebration continued, Miriam, Moses' sister, took up a tambourine and led the women in a joyful dance. The children joined in, their spirits lifted by the music and the infectious joy of the moment. They marveled at the strength and resilience of the people around them, who had endured so much and yet were filled with such hope and gratitude. The children spent time with the Israelites, hearing their stories of hardship and perseverance. They felt a deep sense of admiration for these people who had trusted in God's promise and had been rewarded with freedom. The children understood that this was not just a story of escape but a testament to the enduring power of faith and the unwavering commitment of God to His people.

As the time machine signaled it was time to return home, the children said their goodbyes to the Israelites, feeling honored to have been part of such a historic and miraculous event. They returned to the time machine, their hearts and minds full of the experiences and lessons they had gained. With a final glance at the joyful celebration before them, they set the coordinates for home and stepped inside. The journey back felt reflective, and soon they were standing in their backyard once again. They shared their adventure with their families, recounting the awe-inspiring parting of the Red Sea and the miraculous deliverance of the Israelites. Their families listened with awe and admiration, inspired by the children's stories.

The children decided to document their journey in their journal, filling the pages with detailed drawings and descriptions of the parting of the Red Sea, the walls of water, and the celebration of the Israelites on the far shore. Each page captured a different aspect of their adventure, from the tension of the pursuit to the joy of freedom. As they reflected on their journey, the children realized the importance of faith, resilience, and the power of divine intervention. They understood that the story of the parting of the Red Sea was a powerful testament to God's justice, mercy, and unwavering commitment to His people. Their adventure had taught them valuable lessons about trust, perseverance, and the significance of freedom. They felt a deep connection to the story of Moses and the Israelites and knew that the lessons they had learned would stay with them for a lifetime.

As they settled back into their daily routines, the children looked forward to their next adventure with the time machine. They knew there were countless other stories to discover in the pages of the Bible, each one filled with lessons and insights that would help them grow in their faith and understanding. With each new journey, they felt their bond as friends growing stronger, and their love for discovery deepening. They were a team, a family, and nothing could stop them from exploring the wonders of the past and the lessons they held for the future. With their bond stronger than ever and their love for discovery unquenchable, they were ready to face the world together, one adventure at a time.

They knew that their time machine held many more adventures, and they were eager to see where it would take them next. Whether they were witnessing the creation of the world, the construction of Noah's Ark, the confusion of languages at Babel, God's promises to Abraham, Jacob's divine dream at Bethel, Joseph's dreams and betrayal, his rise to power, the birth of Moses, his encounter with God at the burning bush, the Ten Plagues of Egypt, or the parting of the Red Sea, each journey brought them closer to understanding God's plan and their place in it. They were excited to continue their travels through the pages of history, learning and growing with each new adventure, and they were confident that their time machine would guide them to even more incredible experiences in the future.

Chapter 12 - The Ten Commandments

James, Mary, David, and Linda eagerly gathered around their time machine, ready to embark on another extraordinary adventure. They had witnessed incredible events in the Bible, and now they were setting their coordinates to visit Mount Sinai and witness Moses receiving the Ten Commandments from God. With a familiar hum and flash, they were transported back to the arid, rugged wilderness surrounding Mount Sinai, where they found themselves amidst a vast encampment of Israelites. The air was thick with anticipation and reverence as they approached the foot of the towering mountain. Moses had called the people to prepare themselves, for on the third day, God would descend upon Mount Sinai in a cloud of glory. The children could feel the excitement and awe among the people as they went about their preparations, washing their clothes and purifying themselves for the holy encounter.

On the morning of the third day, the children were awakened by the sound of a loud trumpet blast that echoed through the camp. They hurriedly joined the crowd at the base of the mountain, their eyes wide with wonder as they beheld a scene unlike anything they had ever imagined. Mount Sinai was completely enveloped in smoke because the Lord had descended upon it in fire. The smoke billowed up like smoke from a furnace, and the whole mountain trembled violently. Thunder and lightning flashed across the sky, and the sound of the trumpet grew louder and louder. The children's hearts pounded with a mix of fear and awe as they stood among the Israelites, their faces upturned to the spectacle of God's presence on the mountain.

Moses led the people to the foot of Mount Sinai, where they were instructed to stay at a safe distance and not to approach the mountain. The children watched as Moses, with unwavering faith and determination, ascended the mountain to meet with God. They felt the weight of the moment, understanding that they were about to witness one of the most significant events in biblical history. As Moses climbed higher, the children could see the glow of the divine presence intensify. The mountain quaked, and the sound of the trumpet continued to reverberate through the air. The children held their breath, their eyes fixed on Moses as he disappeared into the thick cloud of smoke and fire.

Inside the cloud, Moses stood before God, his face reflecting the awe and reverence he felt in the presence of the Almighty. The children, though unable to see inside the cloud, could sense the gravity of the encounter. God spoke to Moses, giving him the Ten Commandments that would serve as the foundation of His covenant with the Israelites. The voice of God was powerful and commanding, yet filled with a sense of love and purpose. "I am the Lord your God, who brought you out of Egypt, out of the land of slavery. You shall have no other gods before me. You shall not make for yourself an image in the form of anything in heaven above or on the earth beneath or in the waters below. You shall not bow down to them or worship them; for I, the Lord your God, am a jealous God, punishing the children for the sin of the parents to the third and fourth generation of those who hate me, but showing love to a thousand generations of those who love me and keep my commandments."

The children felt the weight of each commandment as they were delivered, understanding their significance and the moral foundation they provided. "You shall not misuse the name of the Lord your God, for the Lord will not hold anyone guiltless who misuses his name. Remember the Sabbath day by keeping it holy. Six days you shall labor and do all your work, but the seventh day is a Sabbath to the Lord your God. On it you shall not do any work, neither you, nor your son or daughter, nor your male or female servant, nor your animals, nor any foreigner residing in your towns. For in six days the Lord made the heavens and the earth, the sea, and all that is in them, but he rested on the seventh day. Therefore the Lord blessed the Sabbath day and made it holy."

The children could feel the importance of rest and reverence for God in the commandment about the Sabbath. "Honor your father and your mother, so that you may live long in the land the Lord your God is giving you. You shall not murder. You shall not commit adultery. You shall not steal. You shall not give false testimony against your neighbor. You shall not covet your neighbor's house. You shall not covet your neighbor's wife, or his male or female servant, his ox or donkey, or anything that belongs to your neighbor." Each commandment was like a pillar of wisdom and justice, and the children understood that these laws were meant to guide the Israelites in their relationship with God and with one another.

As Moses received the stone tablets inscribed with the Ten Commandments, the children felt a sense of awe and reverence for the divine law being given to humanity. They knew that these commandments would shape the moral and spiritual fabric of the Israelites and influence countless generations to come. Moses began his descent from the mountain, carrying the stone tablets that held the words of God. The children watched as the glow of the divine presence faded and the cloud of smoke and fire began to dissipate. The Israelites, who had been waiting anxiously at the base of the mountain, looked up with anticipation as Moses reappeared, his face radiant from his encounter with God.

As Moses approached the people, the children saw the reverence and awe in the eyes of the Israelites. Moses stood before them, holding the stone tablets high, and proclaimed the words of the covenant that God had made with them. The children listened intently as Moses read the commandments aloud, feeling the weight of the divine law and its implications for the lives of the Israelites. The people responded with a unified voice, committing themselves to obey the commandments and to follow the covenant that God had established with them. The children felt a sense of unity and purpose among the Israelites, understanding that they were bound together by their faith and their commitment to God's law.

The children spent time with the Israelites, learning about their journey from Egypt and the significance of the Ten Commandments in their daily lives. They heard stories of the miracles and trials they had experienced, and they felt a deep connection to the people who had been chosen by God to be His special possession. The children admired the faith and resilience of the Israelites, who had endured so much and yet remained steadfast in their trust in God's promises. As the time machine signaled it was time to return home, the children said their goodbyes to the Israelites, feeling honored to have been part of such a historic and sacred event. They returned to the time machine, their hearts and minds full of the experiences and lessons they had gained. With a final glance at the towering Mount Sinai, they set the coordinates for home and stepped inside.

The journey back felt reflective, and soon they were standing in their backyard once again. They shared their adventure with their families, recounting the awe-inspiring encounter at Mount Sinai and the profound significance of the Ten Commandments. Their families listened with awe and admiration, inspired by the children's stories. The children decided to document their journey in their journal, filling the pages with detailed drawings and descriptions of Mount Sinai, the cloud of smoke and fire, and the stone tablets inscribed with the commandments. Each page captured a different aspect of their adventure, from the thunder and lightning to the divine words that would guide the Israelites.

As they reflected on their journey, the children realized the importance of obedience, faith, and the moral foundation provided by the Ten Commandments. They understood that these laws were not just rules, but a covenant between God and His people, meant to guide them in their relationship with Him and with each other. Their adventure had taught them valuable lessons about justice, reverence, and the enduring power of divine law. They felt a deep connection to the story of Moses and the Israelites and knew that the lessons they had learned would stay with them for a lifetime. As they settled back into their daily routines, the children looked forward to their next adventure with the time machine. They knew there were countless other stories to discover in the pages of the Bible, each one filled with lessons and insights that would help them grow in their faith and understanding.

With each new journey, they felt their bond as friends growing stronger, and their love for discovery deepening. They were a team, a family, and nothing could stop them from exploring the wonders of the past and the lessons they held for the future. With their bond stronger than ever and their love for discovery unquenchable, they were ready to face the world together, one adventure at a time. They knew that their time machine held many more adventures, and they were eager to see where it would take them next. Whether they were witnessing the creation of the world, the construction of Noah's Ark, the confusion of languages at Babel, God's promises to Abraham, Jacob's divine dream at Bethel, Joseph's dreams and betrayal, his rise to power, the birth of Moses, his encounter with God at the burning bush, the Ten Plagues of Egypt, the parting of the Red Sea, or the receiving of the Ten Commandments at Mount Sinai, each journey brought them closer to understanding God's plan and their place in it. They were excited to continue their travels through the pages of history, learning and growing with each new adventure, and they were confident that their time machine would guide them to even more incredible experiences in the future.

Chapter 13 - The Battle of Jericho

James, Mary, David, and Linda were bursting with excitement as they prepared for their next extraordinary adventure. Setting the coordinates on their time machine to witness the legendary Battle of Jericho, they felt the familiar hum and flash as they were transported to ancient Canaan. They found themselves amidst the Israelite camp on the outskirts of Jericho, surrounded by thousands of men, women, and children who were buzzing with anticipation and determination. The massive, fortified city of Jericho loomed in the distance, its high walls casting long shadows over the landscape. The children quickly found Joshua, the resolute leader chosen by God to guide the Israelites into the Promised Land. Joshua welcomed the children warmly and explained the unique strategy God had given him for conquering Jericho. They listened intently as he detailed the plan to march around the city once a day for six days and, on the seventh day, to march around it seven times while the priests blew their trumpets, followed by a loud shout from all the people. Intrigued by the divine strategy, the children eagerly awaited the moment they would witness God's power at work.

On the first day, the children joined the Israelites in their silent march around Jericho. They could feel the tension and curiosity from the inhabitants of Jericho, who watched from the walls. The Israelites moved in unison, led by the priests carrying the Ark of the Covenant, a symbol of God's presence among His people. The only sounds were the shuffling of feet and the occasional blast of the trumpets. The children marveled at the Ark, understanding its significance as a representation of God's guidance and protection. They felt the unity and purpose among the Israelites, who remained silent and focused throughout the march. Each evening, they returned to the camp, filled with anticipation for the days ahead.

For the next five days, the children continued to march with the Israelites around Jericho. The unease among the city's inhabitants grew with each passing day, and the children's excitement and faith in God's plan deepened. They could sense the growing confidence among the Israelites, who were obediently following Joshua's instructions. On the seventh day, the atmosphere was charged with anticipation. The children rose early and joined the Israelites for the final march. This time, they would circle the city seven times. As they began their march, the trumpets blared, and the children felt the intensity of the moment. With each circuit, the anticipation built, and the children could see the determination in the faces of the Israelites.

On the seventh circuit, Joshua gave the command for the people to shout. The children joined in the mighty cry of faith and obedience that echoed across the city. The sound was deafening, filled with the power and determination of thousands of voices united in purpose. Suddenly, the ground beneath them began to tremble, and the walls of Jericho started to crack and crumble. The children watched in awe as the massive walls, once impenetrable, collapsed into rubble. Dust and debris filled the air, and the sound of falling stones mingled with the triumphant shouts of the Israelites. The children could hardly believe their eyes as the fortified city lay in ruins before them.

The Israelites, filled with faith and courage, rushed into the city to claim their victory. The children followed, witnessing the fulfillment of God's promise and the power of His divine intervention. They saw the joy and relief on the faces of the Israelites, who knew that their victory was not by their own strength but by the hand of God. As the dust settled, Joshua commanded that the city and all within it be devoted to the Lord. The children understood the significance of this act, recognizing that the victory at Jericho was a testament to God's faithfulness and the importance of obedience to His commands. They saw Rahab and her family, who had been spared because of her faith and assistance to the Israelite spies, being welcomed into the Israelite camp. The children felt a sense of admiration for Rahab's courage and faith, understanding that her actions had played a crucial role in the victory at Jericho.

The children spent time with the Israelites, listening to their stories of faith and perseverance. They felt a deep connection to the people who had trusted in God's promise and witnessed His miraculous power. The children admired the unity and strength of the Israelites, who had followed Joshua's leadership and remained obedient to God's instructions. As the time machine signaled it was time to return home, the children said their goodbyes to Joshua and the Israelites, feeling honored to have been part of such a historic and miraculous event. They returned to the time machine, their hearts and minds full of the experiences and lessons they had gained. With a final glance at the ruins of Jericho, they set the coordinates for home and stepped inside.

The journey back felt reflective, and soon they were standing in their backyard once again. They shared their adventure with their families, recounting the awe-inspiring events of the Battle of Jericho and the miraculous collapse of the city walls. Their families listened with awe and admiration, inspired by the children's stories. The children decided to document their journey in their journal, filling the pages with detailed drawings and descriptions of the march around Jericho, the blowing of the trumpets, and the walls tumbling down. Each page captured a different aspect of their adventure, from the tension of the march to the joy of victory.

As they reflected on their journey, the children realized the importance of faith, obedience, and the power of divine intervention. They understood that the story of the Battle of Jericho was a powerful testament to God's faithfulness and the significance of trusting in His promises. Their adventure had taught them valuable lessons about perseverance, unity, and the strength that comes from following God's commands. They felt a deep connection to the story of Joshua and the Israelites and knew that the lessons they had learned would stay with them for a lifetime. As they settled back into their daily routines, the children looked forward to their next adventure with the time machine. They knew there were countless other stories to discover in the pages of the Bible, each one filled with lessons and insights that would help them grow in their faith and understanding.

With each new journey, they felt their bond as friends growing stronger, and their love for discovery deepening. They were a team, a family, and nothing could stop them from exploring the wonders of the past and the lessons they held for the future. With their bond stronger than ever and their love for discovery unquenchable, they were ready to face the world together, one adventure at a time. They knew that their time machine held many more adventures, and they were eager to see where it would take them next. Whether they were witnessing the creation of the world, the construction of Noah's Ark, the confusion of languages at Babel, God's promises to Abraham, Jacob's divine dream at Bethel, Joseph's dreams and betrayal, his rise to power, the birth of Moses, his encounter with God at the burning bush, the Ten Plagues of Egypt, the parting of the Red Sea, the receiving of the Ten Commandments at Mount Sinai, or the Battle of Jericho, each journey brought them closer to understanding God's plan and their place in it. They were excited to continue their travels through the pages of history, learning and growing with each new adventure, and they were confident that their time machine would guide them to even more incredible experiences in the future.

Chapter 14 - Gideon's Victory

James, Mary, David, and Linda eagerly gathered around their time machine, ready for another thrilling adventure. This time, they set the coordinates to witness Gideon's miraculous victory over the Midianites. With a familiar hum and flash, they were transported back to ancient Israel, finding themselves in the midst of Gideon's camp at the edge of the Valley of Jezreel. The atmosphere was tense, with the Israelites preparing for an improbable battle against the vast and powerful Midianite army. The children felt the weight of uncertainty and fear among the soldiers, understanding the magnitude of the challenge before them.

Gideon, a humble and unassuming man chosen by God, welcomed the children with a mix of determination and faith. He explained the dire situation: the Midianites, along with the Amalekites and other eastern peoples, had ravaged the land, leaving the Israelites in despair. God had called Gideon to deliver His people, but He had also instructed him to reduce his army from thousands to just 300 men, so that the victory would unmistakably be attributed to God's power and not human strength. The children listened in awe as Gideon recounted how he had tested the soldiers by bringing them to the water and selecting only those who lapped the water with their hands to their mouths.

As night fell, Gideon gathered his small band of 300 men and the children watched in fascination as he revealed his unconventional battle plan. Each man was given a trumpet, an empty jar, and a torch to place inside the jar. Gideon divided the men into three groups, positioning them around the Midianite camp. The children could feel the tension and anticipation in the air as Gideon instructed his men to follow his lead. When the time came, Gideon blew his trumpet and broke his jar, revealing the torch's bright flame. The children watched in awe as the 300 men did the same, their trumpets blasting and the sudden light illuminating the darkness around the Midianite camp.

The Midianites, startled and confused by the noise and lights, were thrown into panic. They mistook the small Israelite force for a vast army and turned on each other in the chaos. The children could hardly believe their eyes as the once formidable Midianite army crumbled in fear and confusion. Gideon's men shouted, "A sword for the Lord and for Gideon!" and the sound echoed through the valley, amplifying the terror among the Midianites. The children followed Gideon and his men as they pursued the fleeing Midianites, witnessing the fulfillment of God's promise and the miraculous victory that had been achieved with only 300 men. They felt a profound sense of awe and gratitude for the divine intervention they had just witnessed.

As the battle concluded, the children joined Gideon and his men in giving thanks to God for the incredible victory. They saw the relief and joy on the faces of the Israelites, who had been delivered from their oppressors in a way that left no doubt about the power and faithfulness of God. The children spent time with Gideon, listening to his reflections on the battle and his deep faith in God's guidance. They felt a deep admiration for Gideon's humility and obedience, understanding that his victory was a testament to the importance of trust and reliance on God's strength rather than one's own.

As the time machine signaled it was time to return home, the children said their goodbyes to Gideon and the Israelites, feeling honored to have been part of such a historic and miraculous event. They returned to the time machine, their hearts and minds full of the experiences and lessons they had gained. With a final glance at the valley where God's power had been so clearly displayed, they set the coordinates for home and stepped inside. The journey back felt reflective, and soon they were standing in their backyard once again. They shared their adventure with their families, recounting the awe-inspiring events of Gideon's victory and the miraculous defeat of the Midianites. Their families listened with awe and admiration, inspired by the children's stories.

The children decided to document their journey in their journal, filling the pages with detailed drawings and descriptions of the battle plan, the trumpets, the torches, and the panic-stricken Midianite camp. Each page captured a different aspect of their adventure, from the tension of the night to the joy of victory. As they reflected on their journey, the children realized the importance of faith, obedience, and the power of divine intervention. They understood that the story of Gideon's victory was a powerful testament to God's faithfulness and the significance of trusting in His promises. Their adventure had taught them valuable lessons about courage, humility, and the strength that comes from following God's commands.

They felt a deep connection to the story of Gideon and the Israelites and knew that the lessons they had learned would stay with them for a lifetime. As they settled back into their daily routines, the children looked forward to their next adventure with the time machine. They knew there were countless other stories to discover in the pages of the Bible, each one filled with lessons and insights that would help them grow in their faith and understanding. With each new journey, they felt their bond as friends growing stronger, and their love for discovery deepening. They were a team, a family, and nothing could stop them from exploring the wonders of the past and the lessons they held for the future.

With their bond stronger than ever and their love for discovery unquenchable, they were ready to face the world together, one adventure at a time. They knew that their time machine held many more adventures, and they were eager to see where it would take them next. Whether they were witnessing the creation of the world, the construction of Noah's Ark, the confusion of languages at Babel, God's promises to Abraham, Jacob's divine dream at Bethel, Joseph's dreams and betrayal, his rise to power, the birth of Moses, his encounter with

God at the burning bush, the Ten Plagues of Egypt, the parting of the Red Sea, the receiving of the Ten Commandments at Mount Sinai, the Battle of Jericho, or Gideon's miraculous victory over the Midianites, each journey brought them closer to understanding God's plan and their place in it. They were excited to continue their travels through the pages of history, learning and growing with each new adventure, and they were confident that their time machine would guide them to even more incredible experiences in the future.

Chapter 15 - Samuel's Call

James, Mary, David, and Linda were brimming with excitement as they gathered around their time machine for yet another remarkable adventure. This time, they set the coordinates to witness the calling of young Samuel by God. With a familiar hum and flash, they were transported back to ancient Israel, arriving at the sacred temple of Shiloh, where they found themselves amidst the tranquil atmosphere of the temple courtyard. The air was filled with a sense of reverence and peace, and they could see the flickering lights of the lamp of God burning near the Ark of the Covenant. The children quietly made their way inside, where they saw young Samuel, a devoted and humble boy, going about his duties under the guidance of Eli, the aging high priest.

As evening fell, the temple grew quiet, and the children found a discreet spot to observe Samuel as he prepared to rest for the night. They could see his dedication and faithfulness in the way he carried out his tasks, tending to the lamp and ensuring everything was in order. Eli, with his frail frame and wise eyes, blessed Samuel and retired to his own room. The children felt a sense of anticipation as they settled in to watch the events unfold. They knew that this night would be a pivotal moment in Samuel's life, one that would set him on a path to becoming one of Israel's greatest prophets.

As Samuel lay down to sleep, the stillness of the night was suddenly broken by a voice calling his name, "Samuel, Samuel." The children saw Samuel sit up, startled and unsure. He quickly ran to Eli's room, thinking the old priest had called him. "Here I am; you called me," Samuel said, his voice filled with innocence and readiness. Eli, puzzled, told Samuel he had not called him and instructed him to return to bed. The children watched as Samuel obediently went back to his room, only to hear the voice calling his name again. "Samuel, Samuel." This time, the children could see the confusion and curiosity in Samuel's eyes as he once again ran to Eli. "Here I am; you called me," he repeated.

Eli, realizing what might be happening, assured Samuel that he had not called him and sent him back to bed.

When the voice called Samuel a third time, the children saw a moment of realization dawn on Eli's face. He understood that it was the Lord calling the boy. He gently instructed Samuel, "Go and lie down, and if he calls you, say, 'Speak, Lord, for your servant is listening.'" The children felt a sense of excitement and awe as Samuel returned to his room, his heart pounding with anticipation. They knew that Samuel was about to have a divine encounter that would change his life forever. As Samuel lay down, the voice called again, "Samuel, Samuel." The children watched in breathless silence as Samuel responded, "Speak, Lord, for your servant is listening." The presence of the Lord filled the room, and the children could feel the holiness and significance of the moment.

God spoke to Samuel, revealing a message of judgment against Eli's family due to the wickedness of his sons and Eli's failure to restrain them. The children could see the weight of the message on Samuel's young shoulders, his face reflecting both the honor of being chosen by God and the gravity of the words he had received. They admired Samuel's courage and humility as he lay quietly, absorbing the profound encounter. As dawn approached, the children followed Samuel as he rose to begin his duties. They could sense his reluctance to share the message with Eli, but they also saw his determination to obey God's call. When Eli called for Samuel, the children watched as the young boy hesitated before finally revealing the Lord's message. Eli, with a mixture of sorrow and acceptance, acknowledged the truth of God's words, saying, "He is the Lord; let him do what is good in his eyes."

The children felt a deep respect for both Samuel and Eli, witnessing their faith and submission to God's will. They spent the rest of the day with Samuel, observing his unwavering dedication to his duties and his growing confidence in his divine calling. They saw how the Lord was with Samuel, and how his words came to be trusted and respected by all of Israel. As the time machine signaled it was time to return home, the children said their goodbyes to Samuel, feeling honored to have witnessed such a significant moment in his life. They returned to the time machine, their hearts and minds full of the experiences and lessons they had gained. With a final glance at the sacred temple of Shiloh, they set the coordinates for home and stepped inside.

The journey back felt reflective, and soon they were standing in their backyard once again. They shared their adventure with their families, recounting the awe-inspiring events of Samuel's call and the divine encounter they had witnessed. Their families listened with awe and admiration, inspired by the children's stories. The children decided to document their journey in their journal, filling the pages with detailed drawings and descriptions of the temple, the moments of Samuel's call, and the solemn exchange with Eli. Each page captured a different aspect of their adventure, from the quiet anticipation of the night to the profound words spoken by God.

As they reflected on their journey, the children realized the importance of listening to God's call, obedience, and the courage to deliver His messages, no matter how difficult they may be. They understood that the story of Samuel's call was a powerful testament to God's faithfulness and the significance of being open and receptive to His voice. Their adventure had taught them valuable lessons about humility, dedication, and the strength that comes from following God's commands. They felt a deep connection to the story of Samuel and Eli and knew that the lessons they had learned would stay with them for a lifetime.

As they settled back into their daily routines, the children looked forward to their next adventure with the time machine. They knew there were countless other stories to discover in the pages of the Bible, each one filled with lessons and insights that would help them grow in their faith and understanding. With each new journey, they felt their bond as friends growing stronger, and their love for discovery deepening. They were a team, a family, and nothing could stop them from exploring the wonders of the past and the lessons they held for the future. With their bond stronger than ever and their love for discovery unquenchable, they were ready to face the world together, one adventure at a time.

They knew that their time machine held many more adventures, and they were eager to see where it would take them next. Whether they were witnessing the creation of the world, the construction of Noah's Ark, the confusion of languages at Babel, God's promises to Abraham, Jacob's divine dream at Bethel, Joseph's dreams and betrayal, his rise to power, the birth of Moses, his encounter with God at the burning bush, the Ten Plagues of Egypt, the parting of the Red Sea, the receiving of the Ten Commandments at Mount Sinai, the Battle of Jericho, Gideon's miraculous victory over the Midianites, or Samuel's divine call, each journey brought them closer to understanding God's plan and their place in it. They were excited to continue their travels through the pages of history, learning and growing with each new adventure, and they were confident that their time machine would guide them to even more incredible experiences in the future.

Chapter 16 - David and Goliath

James, Mary, David, and Linda were filled with excitement as they gathered around their time machine for yet another incredible adventure. This time, they set the coordinates to witness one of the most iconic battles in biblical history: David and Goliath. With a familiar hum and flash, they were transported back to ancient Israel, finding themselves amidst the bustling Israelite camp facing the Philistine army. The air was thick with tension and fear, and the children could see the anxiety in the faces of the soldiers as they gazed across the Valley of Elah at the towering figure of Goliath, the Philistine giant who had been taunting the Israelite army for forty days.

The children made their way through the camp, where they found young David, a shepherd boy who had come to bring food to his brothers serving in King Saul's army. David's eyes were bright with determination and faith as he listened to Goliath's taunts, his heart filled with righteous anger at the giant's defiance of the armies of the living God. The children felt a surge of admiration for David's courage and conviction as he spoke to the men around him, asking what would be done for the man who defeated Goliath. When David's words reached King Saul, the children watched as David was brought before the king. Despite his youth and inexperience as a warrior, David's confidence in God's power was unwavering. "Let no one lose heart on account of this Philistine; your servant will go and fight him," David declared. Saul, initially skeptical, was moved by David's faith and determination. The children felt a thrill of excitement as Saul agreed to let David face Goliath, offering him his own armor. But David, after trying on the heavy armor, chose instead to rely on his simple shepherd's tools: a sling and five smooth stones he picked up from a nearby stream.

The children followed David to the battlefield, their hearts pounding with anticipation. They watched as David approached the

Philistine lines, his figure small and unassuming compared to the towering Goliath, who sneered at the sight of the young boy. "Am I a dog, that you come at me with sticks?" Goliath roared, his voice echoing across the valley. But David, undeterred, responded with unwavering faith. "You come against me with sword and spear and javelin, but I come against you in the name of the Lord Almighty, the God of the armies of Israel, whom you have defied. This day the Lord will deliver you into my hands, and I'll strike you down and cut off your head. This very day I will give the carcasses of the Philistine army to the birds and the wild animals, and the whole world will know that there is a God in Israel."

The children could feel the tension mounting as David and Goliath squared off. They held their breath as David reached into his bag, took out a stone, and placed it in his sling. With a swift, practiced motion, David slung the stone, and the children watched in awe as it flew through the air and struck Goliath squarely on the forehead. The giant's mocking expression turned to shock and disbelief as he staggered and then fell face down to the ground with a thunderous crash. The children erupted in cheers along with the Israelite soldiers, who were galvanized by David's stunning victory. They watched as David ran to Goliath's fallen body, drew the giant's own sword, and cut off his head, holding it high as a symbol of God's deliverance. The Philistine army, seeing their champion defeated, turned and fled in terror, pursued by the jubilant Israelites.

The children followed the victorious army back to the Israelite camp, where they were greeted with cheers and celebrations. They saw King Saul and his general, Abner, marvel at David's bravery and faith. The children felt a deep sense of admiration for David, who had trusted in God's power and triumphed against overwhelming odds. They spent time with David, listening to his reflections on the battle and his unwavering faith in God's guidance. They saw the humility and gratitude in David's eyes as he acknowledged that the victory belonged to the Lord. The children also observed the reactions of David's brothers, who had initially doubted and scorned him but were now filled with pride and respect for their younger sibling.

As the time machine signaled it was time to return home, the children said their goodbyes to David, feeling honored to have witnessed such a historic and miraculous event. They returned to the time machine, their hearts and minds full of the experiences and lessons they had gained. With a final glance at the battlefield where God's power had been so clearly displayed, they set the coordinates for home and stepped inside. The journey back felt reflective, and soon they were standing in their backyard once again. They shared their adventure with their families, recounting the awe-inspiring events of David's victory over Goliath and the miraculous defeat of the Philistine giant. Their families listened with awe and admiration, inspired by the children's stories.

The children decided to document their journey in their journal, filling the pages with detailed drawings and descriptions of the battlefield, the giant Goliath, and David's triumphant stance with the giant's head. Each page captured a different aspect of their adventure, from the tension of the confrontation to the joy of victory. As they reflected on their journey, the children realized the importance of faith, courage, and the power of divine intervention. They understood that the story of David and Goliath was a powerful testament to God's faithfulness and the significance of trusting in His promises. Their adventure had taught them valuable lessons about bravery, humility, and the strength that comes from relying on God's power rather than one's own.

They felt a deep connection to the story of David and knew that the lessons they had learned would stay with them for a lifetime. As they settled back into their daily routines, the children looked forward to their next adventure with the time machine. They knew there were countless other stories to discover in the pages of the Bible, each one filled with lessons and insights that would help them grow in their faith and understanding. With each new journey, they felt their bond as friends growing stronger, and their love for discovery deepening. They were a team, a family, and nothing could stop them from exploring the wonders of the past and the lessons they held for the future.

With their bond stronger than ever and their love for discovery unquenchable, they were ready to face the world together, one adventure at a time. They knew that their time machine held many more adventures, and they were eager to see where it would take them next. Whether they were witnessing the creation of the world, the construction of Noah's Ark, the confusion of languages at Babel, God's promises to Abraham, Jacob's divine dream at Bethel, Joseph's dreams and betrayal, his rise to power, the birth of Moses, his encounter with God at the burning bush, the Ten Plagues of Egypt, the parting of the Red Sea, the receiving of the Ten Commandments at Mount Sinai, the Battle of Jericho, Gideon's miraculous victory over the Midianites, Samuel's divine call, or David's stunning triumph over Goliath, each journey brought them closer to understanding God's plan and their place in it. They were excited to continue their travels through the pages of history, learning and growing with each new adventure, and they were confident that their time machine would guide them to even more incredible experiences in the future.

Chapter 17 - Solomon's Wisdom

James, Mary, David, and Linda gathered around their time machine, excited for their next adventure. They set the coordinates to visit the court of King Solomon, renowned for his extraordinary wisdom. With a familiar hum and flash, they were transported back to ancient Israel, finding themselves amidst the grandeur and splendor of Solomon's palace in Jerusalem. The air was filled with a sense of majesty and reverence, and they could see the hustle and bustle of courtiers, advisors, and petitioners as they made their way through the opulent halls adorned with intricate carvings and gold decorations.

The children marveled at the beauty of the palace and the reverence with which people spoke of King Solomon. They joined a group of petitioners waiting to present their cases before the king. The children felt a sense of anticipation as they watched the proceedings, eager to witness Solomon's legendary wisdom in action. They didn't have to wait long. Soon, a dramatic case was brought before the king: two women, both claiming to be the mother of the same baby. The tension in the room was palpable as the women argued passionately, each insisting that the child was hers.

The children observed Solomon, seated on his magnificent throne, listening intently to the women's pleas. His eyes were calm and thoughtful, and his demeanor exuded authority and compassion. After hearing their arguments, Solomon called for a sword. The children gasped along with the rest of the court as Solomon gave his seemingly shocking order: to divide the living child in two, giving half to each woman. The true mother of the child, her love overcoming her fear, immediately cried out, "Please, my lord, give her the living baby! Don't kill him!" The other woman, however, agreed to the division, revealing her deceit and lack of maternal affection.

The children watched in awe as Solomon, his wisdom piercing through the deception, declared, "Give the living baby to the first woman. Do not kill him; she is his mother." The court erupted in murmurs of admiration and respect, and the children's hearts swelled with admiration for Solomon's keen judgment. They understood that Solomon had used his wisdom to reveal the true mother, protecting the innocent child and delivering justice in a way that left no doubt about his God-given insight. The children spent the day in Solomon's court, witnessing numerous cases and marveling at the king's ability to discern truth and administer justice with fairness and compassion.

They saw how Solomon's wisdom extended beyond judicial matters to encompass governance, diplomacy, and the welfare of his people. The children were impressed by the respect and loyalty Solomon commanded from his subjects and the neighboring nations who sought his counsel. They listened as Solomon discussed matters of state with his advisors, effortlessly weaving wisdom, knowledge, and practical insight into his decisions. The children could see that Solomon's wisdom was a gift from God, enabling him to lead his people with righteousness and understanding.

As the day progressed, the children were granted a private audience with Solomon, who welcomed them with a warm smile. They were struck by his humility and genuine interest in their experiences and questions. Solomon shared with them the story of how he had prayed for wisdom, choosing it over wealth or long life, and how God had blessed him abundantly in return. He encouraged the children to seek wisdom and understanding in their own lives, emphasizing the importance of a discerning heart and a mind open to learning.

The children felt deeply inspired by Solomon's words and the example he set as a wise and just ruler. They admired his dedication to his people and his unwavering commitment to righteousness. They also saw how Solomon's wisdom had a profound impact on the prosperity and peace of Israel, creating a golden age that was admired by other nations. As the time machine signaled it was time to return home, the children said their goodbyes to Solomon, feeling honored to have witnessed his wisdom in action. They returned to the time machine, their hearts and minds full of the experiences and lessons they had gained. With a final glance at the majestic palace, they set the coordinates for home and stepped inside.

The journey back felt reflective, and soon they were standing in their backyard once again. They shared their adventure with their families, recounting the awe-inspiring events of their time in Solomon's court and the miraculous judgments they had witnessed. Their families listened with awe and admiration, inspired by the children's stories. The children decided to document their journey in their journal, filling the pages with detailed drawings and descriptions of Solomon's palace, the dramatic court case of the two mothers, and the wise king's judgments. Each page captured a different aspect of their adventure, from the tension of the courtroom to the profound wisdom of Solomon.

As they reflected on their journey, the children realized the importance of wisdom, justice, and the pursuit of knowledge. They understood that the story of Solomon's wisdom was a powerful testament to God's faithfulness and the significance of seeking His guidance in all things. Their adventure had taught them valuable lessons about discernment, compassion, and the strength that comes from leading with integrity. They felt a deep connection to the story of Solomon and knew that the lessons they had learned would stay with them for a lifetime.

As they settled back into their daily routines, the children looked forward to their next adventure with the time machine. They knew there were countless other stories to discover in the pages of the Bible, each one filled with lessons and insights that would help them grow in their faith and understanding. With each new journey, they felt their bond as friends growing stronger, and their love for discovery deepening. They were a team, a family, and nothing could stop them from exploring the wonders of the past and the lessons they held for the future.

With their bond stronger than ever and their love for discovery unquenchable, they were ready to face the world together, one adventure at a time. They knew that their time machine held many more adventures, and they were eager to see where it would take them next. Whether they were witnessing the creation of the world, the construction of Noah's Ark, the confusion of languages at Babel, God's promises to Abraham, Jacob's divine dream at Bethel, Joseph's dreams and betrayal, his rise to power, the birth of Moses, his encounter with God at the burning bush, the Ten Plagues of Egypt, the parting of the Red Sea, the receiving of the Ten Commandments at Mount Sinai, the Battle of Jericho, Gideon's miraculous victory over the Midianites, Samuel's divine call, David's stunning triumph over Goliath, or Solomon's wise judgments, each journey brought them closer to understanding God's plan and their place in it. They were excited to continue their travels through the pages of history, learning and growing with each new adventure, and they were confident that their time machine would guide them to even more incredible experiences in the future.

As they sat together, planning their next adventure, they felt a deep sense of gratitude for the opportunities they had been given. The children knew that their time machine was more than just a tool for exploring history; it was a gateway to understanding the timeless truths of faith, wisdom, and the human spirit. They were eager to embark on their next journey, ready to discover new stories and learn from the past. With hearts full of anticipation and minds open to new experiences, James, Mary, David, and Linda prepared for their next adventure, knowing that each journey would bring them closer to the heart of God's story and their place within it.

Chapter 18 - Daniel in the Lion's Den

James, Mary, David, and Linda, filled with excitement, gathered around their time machine for another extraordinary adventure. This time, they set the coordinates to witness the story of Daniel in the lion's den. With a familiar hum and flash, they were transported to ancient Babylon, arriving at the bustling city where Daniel, a wise and faithful servant of God, served under King Darius. The children marveled at the grandeur of the city with its towering walls and magnificent palaces, but they were eager to find Daniel and witness his unwavering faith.

As they made their way through the city, they found Daniel in his home, praying and giving thanks to God, as he did three times a day. The children felt a deep sense of admiration for Daniel's devotion and courage, especially knowing the decree that had been issued by King Darius. The decree, influenced by jealous officials, stated that anyone who prayed to any god or human other than the king during the next thirty days would be thrown into the lion's den. Despite the decree, Daniel continued to pray to God openly, and the children could see the peace and strength in his demeanor.

The children followed as the jealous officials spied on Daniel, then hurried to report his actions to King Darius. They watched as the king, distressed by the news, was reminded of the irrevocable law of the Medes and Persians. Despite his respect and fondness for Daniel, the king had no choice but to order Daniel to be thrown into the lion's den. The children saw the sorrow and regret on the king's face as he reluctantly gave the command.

They followed the officials as they led Daniel to the den, a deep pit with a heavy stone cover. The children's hearts pounded with fear and anticipation as they watched Daniel, his faith unwavering, being lowered into the den filled with ferocious lions. They saw the officials place the stone over the opening and seal it with the king's signet ring, ensuring that no one could rescue Daniel. As the night fell, the children could feel the tension in the air. They saw King Darius return to his palace, unable to eat or sleep, worried about his faithful servant.

The children stayed near the den, praying silently for Daniel's safety. They admired his courage and trust in God, even in the face of such a terrifying ordeal. The night seemed endless, but as the first light of dawn began to break, they saw King Darius hurrying to the lion's den, his face filled with hope and anxiety. The children followed closely, their hearts racing with anticipation.

As the king reached the den, he called out in a trembling voice, "Daniel, servant of the living God, has your God, whom you serve continually, been able to rescue you from the lions?" The children held their breath, waiting for a response. To their immense relief and joy, they heard Daniel's calm and steady voice reply, "May the king live forever! My God sent his angel, and he shut the mouths of the lions. They have not hurt me, because I was found innocent in his sight. Nor have I ever done any wrong before you, Your Majesty."

The children watched in awe as the stone was removed and Daniel was lifted out of the den, completely unharmed. They saw the joy and amazement on King Darius's face as he embraced Daniel, praising the God who had delivered him. The children felt a deep sense of wonder and gratitude, witnessing firsthand the power and faithfulness of God.

King Darius immediately ordered the jealous officials and their families to be thrown into the lion's den, where they were quickly devoured, demonstrating the true danger Daniel had faced. The children felt the gravity of the situation and the justice that had been served. King Darius then issued a decree to all the nations and peoples of every language throughout the land, declaring that everyone must fear and reverence the God of Daniel. The children listened as the king proclaimed, "For he is the living God and he endures forever; his kingdom will not be destroyed, his dominion will never end. He rescues and he saves; he performs signs and wonders in the heavens and on the earth. He has rescued Daniel from the power of the lions."

The children spent time with Daniel, listening to his reflections on the miraculous event and his unwavering faith in God. They admired his humility and steadfastness, understanding that his deliverance was a testament to his deep relationship with God. Daniel encouraged the children to always trust in God, no matter the circumstances, and to remain faithful in their prayers and actions.

As the time machine signaled it was time to return home, the children said their goodbyes to Daniel, feeling honored to have witnessed such a profound display of faith and divine protection. They returned to the time machine, their hearts and minds full of the experiences and lessons they had gained. With a final glance at the den where God's power had been so clearly displayed, they set the coordinates for home and stepped inside.

The journey back felt reflective, and soon they were standing in their backyard once again. They shared their adventure with their families, recounting the awe-inspiring events of Daniel's night in the lion's den and the miraculous protection he received. Their families listened with awe and admiration, inspired by the children's stories. The children decided to document their journey in their journal, filling the pages with detailed drawings and descriptions of the lion's den, the fierce lions, and the miraculous deliverance of Daniel. Each page captured a different aspect of their adventure, from the tension of the night to the joy of the morning rescue.

As they reflected on their journey, the children realized the importance of faith, courage, and the power of divine protection. They understood that the story of Daniel in the lion's den was a powerful testament to God's faithfulness and the significance of trusting in His promises. Their adventure had taught them valuable lessons about unwavering faith, the strength that comes from trusting in God, and the importance of remaining steadfast in their beliefs, even in the face of great danger.

They felt a deep connection to the story of Daniel and knew that the lessons they had learned would stay with them for a lifetime. As they settled back into their daily routines, the children looked forward to their next adventure with the time machine. They knew there were countless other stories to discover in the pages of the Bible, each one filled with lessons and insights that would help them grow in their faith and understanding. With each new journey, they felt their bond as friends growing stronger, and their love for discovery deepening. They were a team, a family, and nothing could stop them from exploring the wonders of the past and the lessons they held for the future.

With their bond stronger than ever and their love for discovery unquenchable, they were ready to face the world together, one adventure at a time. They knew that their time machine held many more adventures, and they were eager to see where it would take them next. Whether they were witnessing the creation of the world, the construction of Noah's Ark, the confusion of languages at Babel, God's promises to Abraham, Jacob's divine dream at Bethel, Joseph's dreams and betrayal, his rise to power, the birth of Moses, his encounter with God at the burning bush, the Ten Plagues of Egypt, the parting of the Red Sea, the receiving of the Ten Commandments at Mount Sinai, the Battle of Jericho, Gideon's miraculous victory over the Midianites, Samuel's divine call, David's stunning triumph over Goliath, Solomon's wise judgments, or Daniel's unwavering faith in the lion's den, each journey brought them closer to understanding God's plan and their place in it. They were excited to continue their travels through the pages of history, learning and growing with each new adventure, and they were confident that their time machine would guide them to even more incredible experiences in the future.

As they sat together, planning their next adventure, they felt a deep sense of gratitude for the opportunities they had been given. The children knew that their time machine was more than just a tool for exploring history; it was a gateway to understanding the timeless truths of faith, courage, and the human spirit. They were eager to embark on their next journey, ready to discover new stories and learn from the past. With hearts full of anticipation and minds open to new experiences, James, Mary, David, and Linda prepared for their next adventure, knowing that each journey would bring them closer to the heart of God's story and their place within it.

Chapter 19 – The Romance Of Ruth

James, Mary, David, and Linda gathered around their time machine, eager for another thrilling adventure. This time, they set the coordinates to ancient Moab to witness the story of Ruth, known for her loyalty and faith. With a familiar hum and flash, they were transported back to a dusty road where they saw two women walking side by side. The children quickly realized these were Naomi and her daughter-in-law, Ruth, making their way back to Bethlehem after the death of Naomi's husband and sons. The children's hearts went out to the two women, who were clearly weary and grieving. They joined them, eager to see how Ruth's faith and loyalty would unfold.

As they walked, they listened to Naomi urging Ruth to return to her own family in Moab, saying, "Go back, each of you, to your mother's home. May the Lord show you kindness, as you have shown kindness to your dead husbands and to me." Naomi, full of sorrow, believed there was no future for Ruth in Bethlehem. But Ruth, her heart filled with love and loyalty, responded with a declaration that moved the children deeply. "Don't urge me to leave you or to turn back from you. Where you go I will go, and where you stay I will stay. Your people will be my people and your God my God. Where you die I will die, and there I will be buried. May the Lord deal with me, be it ever so severely, if even death separates you and me."

The children were amazed by Ruth's unwavering commitment to Naomi. They saw Naomi, though still grieving, draw strength from Ruth's words. As they continued their journey, the children noticed the landscape changing from the barren fields of Moab to the fertile lands of Bethlehem. Upon arriving in Bethlehem, the town was abuzz with the news of Naomi's return. The women of the town exclaimed, "Can this be Naomi?" Naomi, whose name means "pleasant," replied, "Don't call me Naomi. Call me Mara, because the Almighty has made my life very bitter. I went away full, but the Lord has brought me back empty."

The children could feel Naomi's pain but also saw the determination in Ruth's eyes to support her mother-in-law. With the barley harvest beginning, Ruth asked Naomi for permission to go to the fields and glean, to gather leftover grain behind anyone in whose eyes she found favor. Naomi agreed, and the children followed Ruth to the fields. They watched as she worked tirelessly, gleaning behind the harvesters, her back bent and hands busy. It was then that they saw Boaz, the owner of the field, a man of standing and relative of Naomi's late husband, Elimelek.

Boaz noticed Ruth and asked his foreman about her. Learning of her loyalty to Naomi, he approached Ruth with kindness. "My daughter, listen to me. Don't go and glean in another field and don't go away from here. Stay here with the women who work for me. Watch the field where the men are harvesting, and follow along after the women. I have told the men not to lay a hand on you. And whenever you are thirsty, go and get a drink from the water jars the men have filled." The children could see Ruth's surprise and gratitude. She bowed down with her face to the ground and asked, "Why have I found such favor in your eyes that you notice me—a foreigner?"

Boaz replied, "I've been told all about what you have done for your mother-in-law since the death of your husband—how you left your father and mother and your homeland and came to live with a people you did not know before. May the Lord repay you for what you have done. May you be richly rewarded by the Lord, the God of Israel, under whose wings you have come to take refuge." The children felt a deep admiration for Boaz's kindness and respect for Ruth's loyalty.

Ruth continued to glean in Boaz's fields until the end of the barley and wheat harvests. Each day, the children observed her hard work and Boaz's continued kindness. Naomi, seeing the favor Ruth had found with Boaz, devised a plan. She instructed Ruth to go to the threshing floor where Boaz would be winnowing barley and to uncover his feet and lie down. Naomi explained that this gesture would signify Ruth's request for Boaz to be her kinsman-redeemer, to marry her and restore their family's fortunes.

The children accompanied Ruth to the threshing floor, their hearts pounding with anticipation. They watched as Ruth quietly uncovered Boaz's feet and lay down. In the middle of the night, Boaz was startled to find a woman at his feet. "Who are you?" he asked. Ruth replied, "I am your servant Ruth. Spread the corner of your garment over me, since you are a guardian-redeemer of our family." Boaz, deeply moved, responded, "The Lord bless you, my daughter. This kindness is greater than that which you showed earlier: You have not run after the younger men, whether rich or poor. And now, my daughter, don't be afraid. I will do for you all you ask. All the people of my town know that you are a woman of noble character."

The children felt a sense of joy and relief as Boaz assured Ruth that he would handle the matter. However, he explained that there was a closer relative who had the first right to redeem. The children followed Boaz to the town gate, where he met with the other relative and ten elders of the town. Boaz explained the situation, and the closer relative declined to redeem, allowing Boaz to take Ruth as his wife.

The children were overjoyed as they witnessed the wedding of Boaz and Ruth, a union that was blessed by God. They saw the love and respect between Boaz and Ruth and the joy it brought to Naomi, whose life was once filled with sorrow. Ruth and Boaz's marriage brought stability and hope to their family. In time, Ruth gave birth to a son named Obed. The children saw the joy old Naomi's eyes as she cradled her grandson, knowing that her family line would continue. They learned that Obed would become the grandfather of King David, establishing Ruth's significant place in the lineage of Jesus.

The children felt deeply inspired by Ruth's loyalty, faith, and the kindness and integrity of Boaz. They admired Naomi's resilience and the way God's hand was evident in their lives, bringing them from sorrow to joy. As the time machine signaled it was time to return home, the children said their goodbyes, feeling honored to have witnessed such a beautiful story of faith and redemption. They returned to the time machine, their hearts and minds full of the experiences and lessons they had gained. With a final glance at the peaceful fields of Bethlehem, they set the coordinates for home and stepped inside.

The journey back felt reflective, and soon they were standing in their backyard once again. They shared their adventure with their families, recounting the touching story of Ruth's loyalty and faith, and the remarkable kindness of Boaz. Their families listened with awe and admiration, inspired by the children's stories. The children decided to document their journey in their journal, filling the pages with detailed drawings and descriptions of the fields of Bethlehem, Ruth gleaning, and the joyous wedding. Each page captured a different aspect of their adventure, from the hardships they witnessed to the happy ending.

As they reflected on their journey, the children realized the importance of loyalty, faith, and the power of God's providence. They understood that the story of Ruth was a powerful testament to the strength of character and the blessings that come from living a life of faith and integrity. Their adventure had taught them valuable lessons about perseverance, kindness, and the importance of trusting in God's plan.

They felt a deep connection to the story of Ruth, Naomi, and Boaz and knew that the lessons they had learned would stay with them for a lifetime. As they settled back into their daily routines, the children looked forward to their next adventure with the time machine. They knew there were countless other stories to discover in the pages of the Bible, each one filled with lessons and insights that would help them grow in their faith and understanding. With each new journey, they felt their bond as friends growing stronger, and their love for discovery deepening. They were a team, a family, and nothing could stop them from exploring the wonders of the past and the lessons they held for the future.

With their bond stronger than ever and their love for discovery unquenchable, they were ready to face the world together, one adventure at a time. They knew that their time machine held many more adventures, and they were eager to see where it would take them next. Whether they were witnessing the creation of the world, the construction of Noah's Ark, the confusion of languages at Babel, God's promises to Abraham, Jacob's divine dream at Bethel, Joseph's dreams and betrayal, his rise to power, the birth of Moses, his encounter with God at the burning bush, the Ten Plagues of Egypt, the parting of the Red Sea, the receiving of the Ten Commandments at Mount Sinai, the Battle of Jericho, Gideon's miraculous victory over the Midianites, Samuel's divine call, David's stunning triumph over Goliath, Solomon's wise judgments, Daniel's unwavering faith in the lion's den, or Ruth's journey of loyalty and faith, each journey brought them closer to understanding God's plan and their place in it. They were excited to continue their travels through the pages of history, learning and growing with each new adventure, and they were confident that their time machine would guide them to even more incredible experiences in the future.

As they sat together, planning their next adventure, they felt a deep sense of gratitude for the opportunities they had been given. The children knew that their time machine was more than just a tool for exploring history; it was a gateway

to understanding the timeless truths of faith, courage, and the human spirit. They were eager to embark on their next journey, ready to discover new stories and learn from the past. With hearts full of anticipation and minds open to new experiences, James, Mary, David, and Linda prepared for their next adventure, knowing that each journey would bring them closer to the heart of God's story and their place within it.

Chapter 20 – Hannah's Help

James, Mary, David, and Linda gathered around their time machine, excited for their next adventure. This time, they set the coordinates to ancient Israel to witness the story of Hannah, a woman known for her heartfelt prayers and unwavering faith. With a familiar hum and flash, they were transported back to the ancient town of Shiloh, where they found themselves amidst a bustling crowd heading towards the tabernacle. The children saw a woman walking quietly, her face a mix of sorrow and determination. They quickly recognized her as Hannah, the wife of Elkanah, who was deeply distressed because she had no children.

The children followed Hannah as she made her way through the crowd. They could feel her sadness and longing, especially as they saw another woman, Peninnah, Elkanah's other wife, with her many children, taunting and provoking Hannah. Despite her husband Elkanah's love and attempts to comfort her, Hannah could not be consoled. Her deep desire for a child consumed her thoughts and prayers. As they approached the tabernacle, the children saw Hannah slip away to a quiet corner to pray.

Kneeling on the ground, Hannah poured out her heart to God, tears streaming down her face. The children listened as she made a solemn vow, "Lord Almighty, if you will only look on your servant's misery and remember me, and not forget your servant but give her a son, then I will give him to the Lord for all the days of his life, and no razor will ever be used on his head." They felt the intensity of her plea and the depth of her faith. As she prayed silently, moving her lips but making no sound, Eli the priest noticed her and thought she was drunk. He approached her and said, "How long are you going to stay drunk? Put away your wine."

Hannah, her voice steady despite her tears, replied, "Not so, my lord. I am a woman who is deeply troubled. I have not been drinking wine or beer; I was pouring out my soul to the Lord. Do not take your servant for a wicked woman; I have been praying here out of my great anguish and grief." The children watched as Eli, realizing his mistake, responded with kindness and assurance. "Go in peace, and may the God of Israel grant you what you have asked of him."

Hannah left the tabernacle with a renewed sense of hope and peace, her faith strengthened by Eli's words. The children could see a change in her demeanor as she rejoined Elkanah and the rest of the family. She was no longer downcast, but filled with quiet confidence that God had heard her prayer. Time passed, and the children continued to observe Hannah and Elkanah as they returned to their home in Ramah. They watched with anticipation as Hannah's belly began to swell, signaling the answer to her fervent prayers. The joy in the household was palpable when Hannah gave birth to a son, whom she named Samuel, saying, "Because I asked the Lord for him."

The children felt a deep sense of joy and awe at witnessing the fulfillment of Hannah's heartfelt prayers. They saw the love and devotion Hannah poured into raising Samuel during his early years. She never forgot her vow to God and cherished every moment with her son, knowing that the time would come when she would have to fulfill her promise. When Samuel was old enough, Hannah prepared to take him to Shiloh to dedicate him to the Lord's service. The children joined the journey back to the tabernacle, feeling the bittersweet mix of emotions Hannah must have felt. They saw her and Elkanah bring sacrifices and offerings to the tabernacle as a sign of their gratitude and commitment.

Standing before Eli, Hannah reminded him of their previous encounter, saying, "Pardon me, my lord. As surely as you live, I am the woman who stood here beside you praying to the Lord. I prayed for this child, and the Lord has granted me what I asked of him. So now I give him to the Lord. For his whole life he will be given over to the Lord." The children watched as Hannah placed young Samuel in Eli's care, a look of pride and sadness mingling on her face. They admired her strength and faith, knowing how difficult it must have been to fulfill her vow.

The children saw Hannah and Elkanah return to Ramah, their hearts full of gratitude and trust in God's plan. They knew that Hannah's faith and dedication would be richly rewarded. Over the years, they saw Hannah visit Samuel at the tabernacle, bringing him a little robe she made each year. They felt the love and pride in her eyes as she watched her son grow in the service of the Lord, under Eli's guidance. Samuel grew to be a great prophet and leader in Israel, his life a testament to the power of a mother's prayer and the faithfulness of God.

The children also saw how God blessed Hannah and Elkanah with more children – three sons and two daughters – as a sign of His continued favor and faithfulness. Hannah's story, marked by her deep faith and unwavering trust in God, left a profound impact on the children. As the time machine signaled it was time to return home, they said their goodbyes to Hannah, feeling honored to have witnessed her journey of faith and dedication. They returned to the time machine, their hearts and minds full of the experiences and lessons they had gained. With a final glance at the peaceful town of Ramah, they set the coordinates for home and stepped inside.

The journey back felt reflective, and soon they were standing in their backyard once again. They shared their adventure with their families, recounting the moving story of Hannah's heartfelt prayers and the miraculous birth of Samuel. Their families listened with awe and admiration, inspired by the children's stories. The children decided to document their journey in their journal, filling the pages with detailed drawings and descriptions of Hannah's prayers, the birth of Samuel, and the dedication at the tabernacle. Each page captured a different aspect of their adventure, from the anguish of Hannah's prayers to the joy of Samuel's birth and dedication.

As they reflected on their journey, the children realized the importance of faith, perseverance, and the power of prayer. They understood that the story of Hannah was a powerful testament to God's faithfulness and the significance of trusting in His promises. Their adventure had taught them valuable lessons about the strength that comes from unwavering faith and the blessings that follow sincere devotion and trust in God's plan.

They felt a deep connection to the story of Hannah and Samuel and knew that the lessons they had learned would stay with them for a lifetime. As they settled back into their daily routines, the children looked forward to their next adventure with the time machine. They knew there were countless other stories to discover in the pages of the Bible, each one filled with lessons and insights that would help them grow in their faith and understanding. With each new journey, they felt their bond as friends growing stronger, and their love for discovery deepening. They were a team, a family, and nothing could stop them from exploring the wonders of the past and the lessons they held for the future.

With their bond stronger than ever and their love for discovery unquenchable, they were ready to face the world together, one adventure at a time. They knew that their time machine held many more adventures, and they were eager to see where it would take them next. Whether they were witnessing the creation of the world, the construction of Noah's Ark, the confusion of languages at Babel, God's promises to Abraham, Jacob's divine dream at Bethel, Joseph's dreams and betrayal, his rise to power, the birth of Moses, his encounter with God at the burning bush, the Ten Plagues of Egypt, the parting of the Red Sea, the receiving of the Ten Commandments at Mount Sinai, the Battle of Jericho, Gideon's miraculous victory over the Midianites, Samuel's divine call, David's stunning triumph over Goliath, Solomon's wise judgments, Daniel's unwavering faith in the lion's den, Ruth's journey of loyalty and faith, or Hannah's heartfelt prayers for a child, each journey brought them closer to understanding God's plan and their place in it. They were excited to continue their travels through the pages of history, learning and growing with each new adventure, and they were confident that their time machine would guide them to even more incredible experiences in the future.

As they sat together, planning their next adventure, they felt a deep sense of gratitude for the opportunities they had been given. The children knew that their time machine was more than just a tool for exploring history; it was a gateway to understanding the timeless truths of faith, courage, and the human spirit. They were eager to embark on their next journey, ready to discover new stories and learn from the past. With hearts full of anticipation and minds open to new experiences, James, Mary, David, and Linda prepared for their next adventure, knowing that each journey would bring them closer to the heart of God's story and their place within it.

Conclusion

As we reach the conclusion of "The Time Machine Chronicles: Old Testament Characters," we reflect on the incredible journey that James, Mary, David, and Linda have experienced. Through the lens of time travel, these four children have not only witnessed the lives of iconic biblical figures but have also internalized the deep spiritual lessons that these stories convey. Their adventures through the ancient world have left a lasting impact on them, transforming their understanding of faith, trust, courage, and forgiveness.

James, who began his journey struggling with doubt and uncertainty, found his faith strengthened as he witnessed Noah's unwavering trust in God while building the ark. The lesson he learned—that God's plans are always worth following, even when they seem impossible—gave him the confidence to trust in God's guidance in his own life. James returns from his journey with a renewed sense of faith, understanding that true trust in God can move mountains and bring about incredible outcomes.

Mary, in her search for meaning and purpose, was deeply moved by Abraham and Sarah's story. Seeing God fulfill His promises to them despite all odds taught her that patience and faith are key in waiting for God's timing. She learned that God's plans for her life are both purposeful and fulfilling, even if the path isn't immediately clear. Mary now carries with her the reassurance that God's promises never fail, and that her purpose will unfold in His perfect timing.

David, who grappled with fear and anxiety, found his courage in the story of young David facing Goliath. Witnessing the biblical David's bravery and trust in God's power inspired him to confront his own fears, knowing that with God by his side, no challenge is too great to overcome. The experience gave David a newfound confidence to tackle the obstacles in his life, armed with the knowledge that God is always with him.

Linda's struggle with forgiveness was transformed by the story of Joseph. Observing Joseph's ability to forgive his brothers despite their betrayal showed her the power of letting go of bitterness and embracing forgiveness. Linda learned that forgiveness is not just about freeing others, but also about freeing herself from the burden of anger and resentment. Her heart was softened as she understood that forgiveness leads to healing and that God's grace is sufficient to mend even the deepest wounds.

As their journey through the Old Testament comes to an end, James, Mary, David, and Linda return to their own time with a treasure trove of wisdom and a deeper relationship with God. Their adventures have shown them that the stories of the Bible are not just ancient tales, but living lessons that continue to speak to us today. These experiences have equipped them—and hopefully, you as well—with the tools needed to face life's challenges with faith, courage, and trust in God's unfailing promises.

"The Time Machine Chronicles: Old Testament Characters" is a testament to the enduring power of Scripture and the timeless truths it contains. Just as James, Mary, David, and Linda have been transformed by their journey, may you too be inspired to explore the Bible with fresh eyes, allowing its stories to guide and shape your walk with God. Remember, the lessons of the Old Testament are not confined to the past—they are alive and active, ready to guide you through every step of your spiritual journey. As you close this book, may you carry with you the lessons learned and the conviction that, with God, all things are possible.

Don't miss out!

Visit the website below and you can sign up to receive emails whenever Joshua Rhoades publishes a new book. There's no charge and no obligation.

https://books2read.com/r/B-A-AJLBB-WZBYE

BOOKS 2 READ

Connecting independent readers to independent writers.

Did you love *The Time Machine Chronicles: Old Testament Characters*? Then you should read *Consider The Ant - God's Tiny Preachers*[1] by Joshua Rhoades!

[2]

In the vast and intricate world of creation, God has embedded profound lessons within the smallest of creatures, urging us to look beyond the obvious and consider the wisdom of the ant. In "Consider The Ant - God's Tiny Preachers," we look into the remarkable world of ants, those tiny but powerful teachers, whose lives reflect spiritual truths that can profoundly impact our walk with God. Proverbs 6:6 beckons us to "Go to the ant, thou sluggard; consider her ways, and be wise:" a call to observe and emulate the diligence, unity, and perseverance exemplified by these seemingly insignificant insects. Each type of ant, from the tireless worker to the vigilant soldier, reveals a facet of the Christian life, offering us insights into how we can better serve, protect, and and lead. The worker ant, with its relentless dedication to gathering food and caring for the colony, mirrors the Christian's call to service, reminding us that no task in God's kingdom is too small or insignificant. The soldier ant, ever on guard to defend

1. https://books2read.com/u/mB7LXR

2. https://books2read.com/u/mB7LXR

the colony, symbolizes the Christian's role in spiritual warfare, standing firm in the faith and safeguarding the truths of the gospel. Meanwhile, the queen ant, the heart of the colony, quietly embodies leadership and purpose, reflecting the importance of fulfilling our God-given roles with grace and dedication. Finally, the ant colony as a whole serves as a powerful metaphor for the local church, where each member, no matter how small, contributes to honoring the Lord, creating a thriving, harmonious body that mirrors the unity and effectiveness God desires for His church. As we explore these tiny preachers throughout this book, may we be inspired to embrace the lessons they offer, applying them to our lives so that we, too, may walk in wisdom, diligence, and unity, fulfilling our divine purpose in the grand design of God's kingdom.